Systems in Motion
Exploring Complexity through an Interdisciplinary Lens

LEVEL B

Part of a three-level series

Level A (for ages 5 and up)

Level B (for ages 8 and up)

Level C (for ages 13 and up)

by Jennifer Andersen and Anne LaVigne
in collaboration with the Creative Learning Exchange

Creative Learning Exchange
Acton, Massachusetts
2014

DEDICATION

To Jay Forrester
for his tireless commitment to making the world a better place
through empowering young people to better understand the complexity around
them and make a positive difference in their own and others' lives.

ACKNOWLEDGEMENTS

This book was created through the efforts, encouragement, and
support of many and is the culmination of learning gained from years of
collaboration with more people than we could possibly name. In addition to
being grateful to our loving families and to each and every person who
helped us along the journey, special thanks goes to those directly
involved in the review, editing, and final project completion:

Jan Bramhall
Joanne Egner
Marcy Kenah
Bunny Lawton

Michael Radzicki
George Richardson
Amanda Wait

Funding was made possible through the generosity of Jay Forrester.

Table of Contents

Getting Started — 7

    Introduction — 9

    Simulations and Lessons — 9

    Implementation Guidelines — 10

    Materials and Logistics — 11

Simulations and Lessons — 13

Level B Lessons (for ages 8 and up)

    Exploring Springs: A Little Bounce in the World — 15

    Romeo and Juliet: Parallel Universe — 23

    Why Are There Not More Elephants? Population Dynamics — 35

    Wild Things: Interacting Populations — 45

    Circles of Interaction: Predator, Prey and Plants — 57

    Running in Circles: How Fast Can We Go? — 75

    From Farm to Table: The Ups and Downs of What We Buy — 97

Everything Else — 113

    Appendix A: Characteristics of Complex Systems — 115

    Appendix B: System Dynamics Visual Tools — 117

    Appendix C: Technical Matters — 118

Getting Started

"Every thought tends to connect something with something else, to establish a relation between things. Every thought moves, grows and develops, fulfills a function, solves a problem."

Lev S. Vygotsky, *Thought and Language*

Introduction

This series of seven interdisciplinary lessons with accompanying free, online simulations has explicit connections to curriculum content standards and to critical thinking skills.

Simulations also illustrate how perceived problems or undesirable behavior can arise from the structure of a system itself, as opposed to outside influences. A system with many ups and downs behaves in that manner because it has an inherent tendency to do so. For example, the very nature of a spring is to bounce up and down, not due to some outside force, but because its structure causes it to do so.

Simulations and Lessons

Each simulation creates an open, engaging environment for students to explore guided and self-generated questions, while gaining content knowledge.

Level of the materials

Most simulation contexts have three levels – A, B, and C. These levels correspond, in general, to different ages:

    Level A – Ages 5 and up
    Level B – Ages 8 and up
    Level C – Ages 13 and up

In addition, since the levels share the same underlying context, a teacher may find using different levels appropriate for differentiation of instruction.

This book contains only the Level B lessons and handouts, other books in the series include materials for the other two levels, A and C.

Connections to curriculum standards

Although the lesson contexts may initially seem focused on a particular subject area, each of the simulations relates to curriculum standards across multiple contexts. The table (Figure 1) illustrates simulation contexts, available levels, and curricular connections.

Lesson Context	Description	Levels			Curricular Connections					
		A	B	C	Engineering	Language Arts	Math	Science	Social Studies	Social/ Emotional
Spring	See how a spring (e.g., a Slinky®) moves when changing its structure and environment.	√	√	√	√	√	√	√		
Relationships	Explore relationships on the playground (A) and in literature (B and C)	√	√	√		√	√	√	√	√
Population	Watch animal populations increase up to a limiting carrying capacity.	√	√	√		√	√	√		
Predator/Prey	Investigate a relationship between predator and prey populations, based on a real island ecosystem.	√	√	√		√	√	√		
Predator/Prey/ Food	Take on the role of wildlife manager to see how the availability of food for prey affects the whole system.	√	√	√		√	√	√		
Burnout	Become a peer advisor, helping students find solutions to burnout cycles.		√	√		√	√	√	√	√
Commodities	Write an article as a journalist investigating different farming practices, while learning about commodity cycles.		√	√		√	√	√	√	

FIGURE 1: Simulations and Context Connections

Implementation Guidelines

These are general guidelines for using the simulations with accompanying lessons and handouts. Each lesson includes suggestions for introducing, implementing, debriefing, and assessing a simulation. Teachers are free to adapt the materials for their own use to meet the needs of their students.

Level of guidance

The simulations allow students to work interdependently with a partner, while following prompts on the screen and within the handouts. Depending on individual and class needs, the teacher may need to provide additional whole-class or small group guidance throughout the simulation experience.

Omit some or all of the handouts, based on instructional goals and depending on student age, reading ability, and level of self-direction. One option is to create a flexible, more 'organic' environment for students to explore the simulations, along with alternate methods for students to demonstrate understanding.

Making predictions and comparing results

The use of dynamic simulations opens possibilities for students to make predictions, design simple experiments, and compare actual results to predicted behavior. These tasks are connected to multiple curricular standards and also enhance students' ability to think deeply about what is causing particular results. The handouts guide students through this process, but conversations before and after the simulation can help students practice the critical thinking skill of evaluating interdependent relationships within a dynamic system.

Assessing student learning

Assessment can take place informally through small group/class conversations and formally through simulation handouts, independently completed written assessments, and oral presentations.

Informal assessment: As students work through the simulations, observe the kinds of conversations they have. For example, to what degree are they able to describe cause-and-effect connections among the parts? For this reason, having students work within a group of 2-3 students encourages collaborative decision-making and reflection as they experience simulation results. While 'floating' through the classroom to observe student progress, ask students open-ended questions about discoveries and insights gained.

Formal assessment: The lessons include handouts, assessments, and suggested projects. Although example student responses for some handout questions are included within lesson plans, no official answer keys are provided. Most questions allow for multiple "correct" answers. Some questions seek an opinion, inference, or interpretation, along with evidence. These questions, by their very nature, do not lend themselves to the creation of a discrete set of answers.

Materials and Logistics

Very little, in terms of supplies, preparation, and materials is needed for implementation.

Printing the handouts

Unless otherwise indicated, handouts are formatted for double-sided printing. Some handouts are optional, depending on prior student experience. For example, one lesson includes a handout based on having read a particular book.

Materials

All that's needed are one or more computers with Internet access and the lessons with accompanying handouts. At the time of this printing, the simulations will not work on iPhone or iPad devices unless a separate flash-capable browser app is purchased and installed. They will work on many other portable tablets. *Note*: if only one computer is available, one option is to project the simulation and use it as a whole-class activity/discussion. For each run, ask students to propose settings, run the simulation, and discuss as a class.

Accessing the simulations

All simulations are available online at no cost from The Creative Learning Exchange via the QR code or at:

https://exchange.iseesystems.com/profile/25/52

All Simulations

Time

Each lesson gives a general guideline for completion time, generally three to four 45-minute class periods to introduce, use the simulation, and debrief the experience. The actual time needed to complete any particular simulation will vary based on individual and classroom differences. Feel free to adjust the amount of time, based on instructional goals.

Last word

How easy is this…really? It's just as simple as opening the link to one of the simulations. The handouts can guide students, so they don't miss parts of the simulation content, but students can also gain new insights through a more organic exploration of the simulations. No one right way exists to use these resources. Explore, discover, and enjoy together with your students!

Simulations & Lessons

"The intuitively obvious 'solutions' to social problems are apt to fall into one of several traps set by the character of complex systems."

Jay W. Forrester, *World Dynamics*

PHOTO BY ANNE LAVIGNE

Lesson 1 – Level B
Exploring Springs: A Little Bounce in the World

Overview

Students explore a simple spring simulation to see how springs behave, given different characteristics. Students can change the springiness, the resistance, a mass at the end of the spring, and the amount of push or pull.

Learning goals

- Represent and interpret data on a line graph.
- Compare/contrast how different types of springs behave based on specific characteristics.
- Match a spring's description to an accompanying graph.
- Identify and describe other examples that oscillate in a similar fashion as a spring.

FIGURE 1: Title Screen

Student Challenge

Create different types of springs that behave in different ways – largest change in position, fastest oscillation, slowest oscillation, etc.

LESSON 1 – LEVEL B – AGES 8+

Time
Two 45-minute sessions

Materials
- One computer for every 2–3 students
- Handout (See pages 18–21)
- Slinky® or other springs

Curricular Connections
- Equilibrium is the physical state in which forces and changes occur in opposite and offsetting directions.
- The motion of an object can be described by its position, direction of motion, and speed. That motion can be measured and represented on a graph.
- Math: Look for and make use of structure, analyze patterns and relationships, and represent and interpret data*

Common Core State Standards

Key system dynamics concepts and insights
- Springs move as they do because of how they are made; they have the potential to oscillate but can be at rest.
- Movement is affected by characteristics such as mass and "springiness."
- A behavior-over-time graph can show the physical movement of a spring.

Additional information, based on Level C simulation

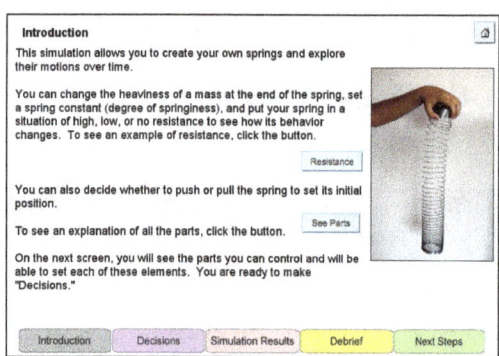

FIGURE 2: Introduction

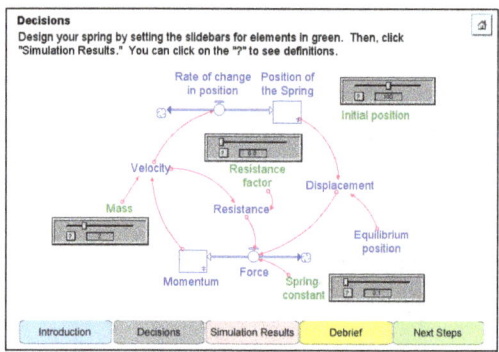

FIGURE 3: Make Decisions

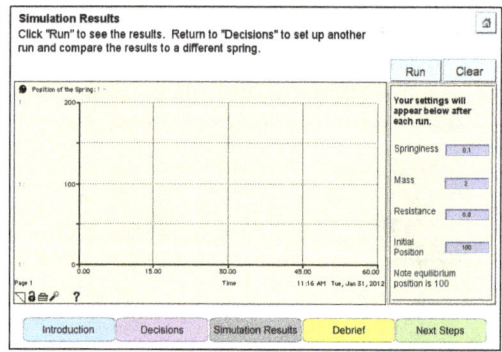

FIGURE 4: Simulation Results

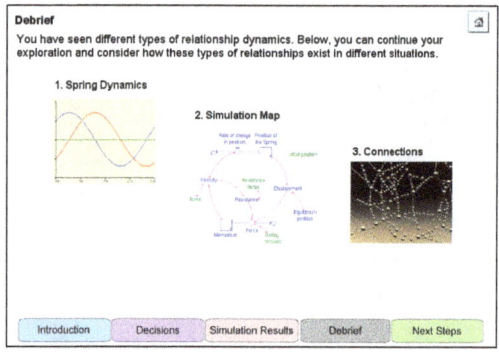

FIGURE 5: Debrief

Lesson Details

Preparation

1. Create groups of 2–3 students each.
2. Copy included handouts for each student group.
3. Check computers to make sure you can access the simulation.

Session 1

1. Introduce students to springs and the key concepts in the simulation as needed. Note that students can also explore these concepts within both the introduction and debrief. If possible, have actual springs for students to explore (e.g., a Slinky®). Key concepts include:

   a. **Spring Constant (or Springiness)** – How easy is the spring to pull apart? How might the spring behave if it were really hard to pull? Really easy?

   b. **Position** – What does the position of a spring refer to? What point are we measuring? [Note that the height of the bottom of the spring from the floor is the point being measured in the simulation.]

   c. **Initial Position** – How can you move the spring before releasing it? What will happen if we push it up? Pull it down? Where would the graph start on the y-axis for each of these cases?

   d. **Mass** – You will place an object at the bottom of the spring. The mass of the object is measured in kilograms (kg). How might the spring behave with a small mass? Large mass?

   e. **Resistance** – Is there anything that slows down the spring? Does air slow down the spring? What would happen to the spring if it were in a no-gravity environment?

   f. Optional terms to consider, depending on curricular goals, include momentum, force, and velocity.

2. Have students open the simulation, read the introduction, and view the parts of the simulation on the "Introduction" screen (Figure 2).

3. Have students record data on the handouts as they explore different springs, and compare the resulting trends (Figures 3 and 4). You may want to have students set up one spring and then do further experiments while changing only one element at a time.

4. After they have completed the desired number of simulation runs, students can begin working on the comparison handout, representing all the springs on one graph.

Session 2

1. If needed, have students complete the simulation within their small groups.
2. After running the simulation multiple times, students can continue to the "Debrief" section (Figure 5).
3. Debrief the simulation experience using ideas for bringing the lesson home, assessment, and "Next Steps" (Figure 6).

Bringing the Lesson Home

- Have students explore the "Debrief" section of the simulation within their small group or as a class.
- Consider why the springs always oscillated except in the case when starting in equilibrium.
- Discuss how to create different types of spring behavior – faster oscillations, slower oscillations, damped oscillations, etc.

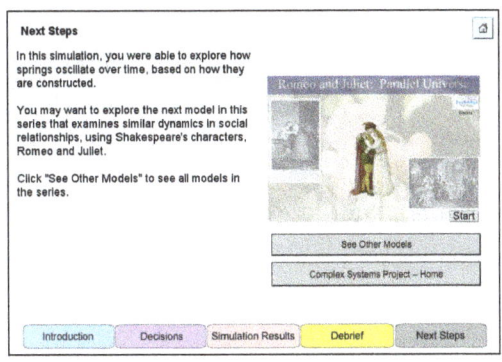

FIGURE 6: Next Steps

Assessment Ideas

- Use Assessment 1 to have students identify how different graphs match different spring descriptions.
- Use Assessment 2 to have students describe the parts of the model and the loops embedded within the simulation.

Note: Assessment Handouts 1 and 2 can be formative or summative assessments.

Assessment 1 answers:

1. Graph 1, Graph 2
2. Graph 2, Graph 1
3. Graph 2, Graph 1
4. Graph 1, Graph 2

ACKNOWLEDGEMENTS

Lesson 1 – Level B • Exploring Springs: A Little Bounce in the World ©2014 Creative Learning Exchange www.clexchange.org

This model with accompanying lesson is one in a series that explores the characteristics of complex systems.

Model created with contributions from Jen Andersen, Anne LaVigne, Michael Radzicki, George Richardson, Lees Stuntz, with support from Jay Forrester and the Creative Learning Exchange.

Image Credits
Slinky front screen, boy with slinky, hands holding slinkys, hands holding glass - Photographs and video by LaVigne.
Animated springs - Oleg Alexadrov, Wikimedia Commons, Public Domain.
Butterfly - Bilboq, Wikimedia Commons, Public Domain.
Food - Daderot, Wikimedia Commons, Public Domain.
Swing - Dimitri Nyet, Wikimedia Commons, Public Domain.
Lion – Trisha M. Shears, Wikimedia Commons, Public Domain.
Dicentra hearts (flowers), Rob Hille, Wikimedia Commons, Public Domain.

Color photolithograph of Romeo/Juliet, Toy Theater print document, Wikimedia Commons, Public Domain.
Engraving of Romeo and Juliet with group, painting by William Miller, engraving by A. Smith, Wikimedia Commons, Public Domain.
Romeo and Juliet by balcony, painting by John Francis Rigaud, engraving by James Stow, Wikimedia Commons, Public Domain.
Spider Web, US Fish and Wildlife Service, Public Domain

LESSON 1, LEVEL B, HANDOUT – P.1

Exploring Springs Simulation

Use the handout to design springs and record your results. For each spring, first draw your prediction on the graph showing the spring's position over time. Then run and record the actual behavior of the spring.

Spring #_____

Mass	
Spring constant	
Resistance factor	
Initial Position	

Spring #_____

Mass	
Spring constant	
Resistance factor	
Initial Position	

Spring #_____

Mass	
Spring constant	
Resistance factor	
Initial Position	

LESSON 1, LEVEL B, HANDOUT – P.2

Spring Comparisons
Create a key for the springs and draw the trends on the graph below.

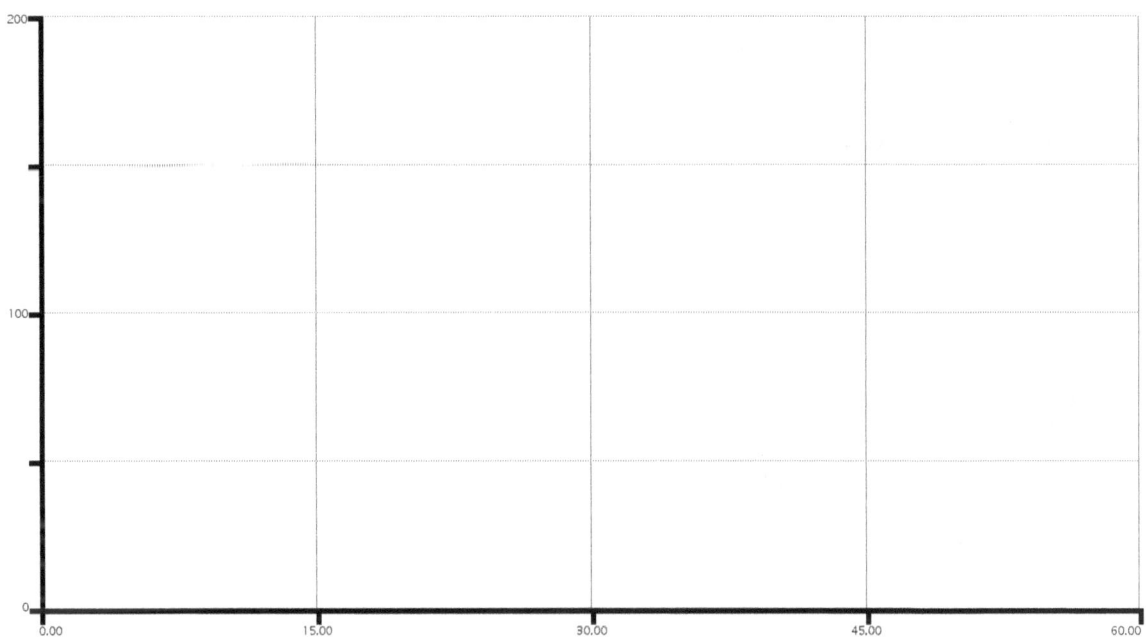

How are the trends similar and different?
_____
_____
_____

Using vocabulary from the simulation, explain why the spring behaviors are similar.
_____
_____
_____

Why are they different?
_____
_____
_____

Assessment 1
Look at the spring descriptions below. Match each description to a graph that is the closest match.

1. A spring with a high spring constant more closely matches Graph # ____.

   A spring with a low spring constant more closely matches Graph # ____.

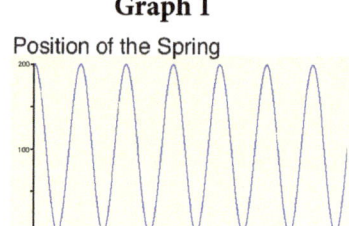
Graph 1

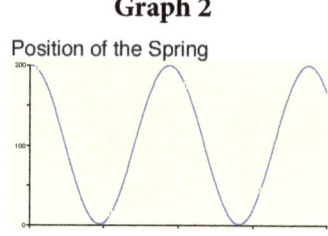
Graph 2

2. A spring with low resistance more closely matches Graph # ____.

   A spring with high resistance more closely matches Graph # ____.

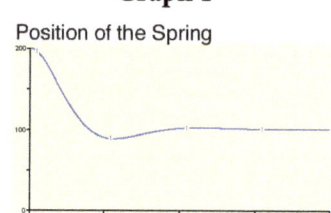
Graph 1

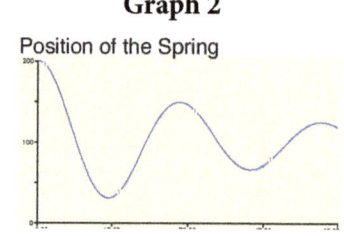
Graph 2

3. A spring with low mass attached more closely matches Graph # ____.

   A spring with high mass attached more closely matches Graph # ____.

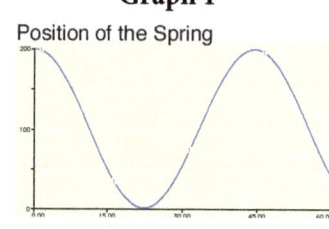
Graph 1

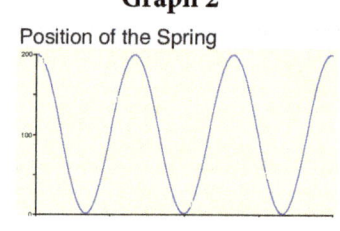
Graph 2

4. A spring with high resistance and a high spring constant more closely matches Graph # ____.

   A spring with low resistance and a low spring constant more closely matches Graph # ____.

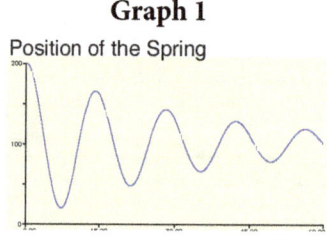
Graph 1

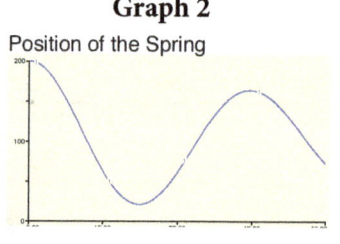
Graph 2

LESSON 1, LEVEL B, HANDOUT – P.4

Assessment 2
Look at the map below. Describe the parts and how they impacted the spring's position over time.

Resistance: _____
_____
_____

Mass: _____
_____
_____

Initial Position: _____
_____
_____

Spring Constant: _____
_____
_____

Using the Word Bank below, describe the spring you would design to see the resulting position graph.

Word Bank:
position   initial position

resistance   time

mass   spring constant

spring

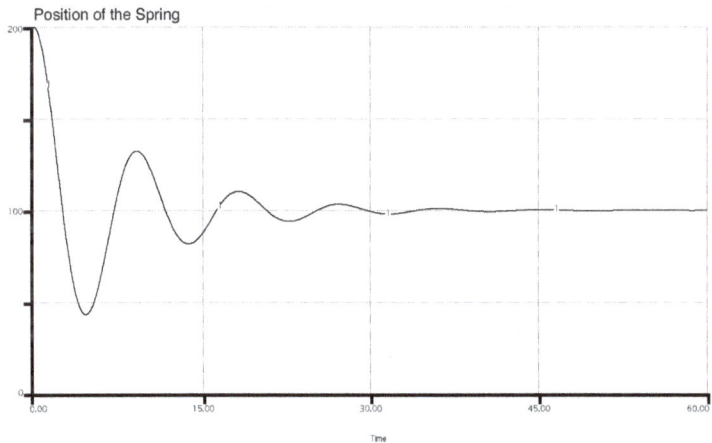

_____
_____
_____
_____
_____

©2014 Creative Learning Exchange   LESSON 1 – Level B • Exploring Springs • 21

Lesson 2 – Level B

Romeo and Juliet: Parallel Universe

Overview

Students use a simple simulation to explore "What if" questions relating to characters. They can change how characters behave to consider whether a story might have emerged differently. Note that students do not need to read the play, *The Tragedy of Romeo and Juliet*, in order to explore the simulation.

Learning goals

- Represent and interpret data on a line graph.
- Create conditions that produce specific relationship dynamics.
- Describe a loop of feelings between two characters.
- Identify and describe other types of relationships that oscillate in a similar fashion.

FIGURE 1: Title Screen

Student Challenge

Create different scenarios for the relationship between Romeo and Juliet – one that they perceive as matching the original story dynamics and others that are variations.

LESSON 2 – LEVEL B – AGES 8+

Time
Two 45-minute sessions

Materials
- One computer for every 2–3 students
- Handout (See pages 27–34)

Curricular Connections
- Language Arts: Analyze how particular elements of a story or drama interact.*
- Language Arts: Compare and contrast a written story, drama, or poem to its audio, filmed, staged, or multimedia version, analyzing the effects of techniques unique to each medium.*

Common Core State Standards

Key system dynamics concepts and insights
- Social systems are complex and we can use models and simulation to explore social relationships.
- Social systems may demonstrate similar trends as are seen within other systems, such as mechanical or ecological systems.

Additional information, based on Level C simulation

©2014 Creative Learning Exchange

Lesson Details

Preparation

1. Create groups of 2–3 students each.
2. Copy included handouts for each student or student group.
3. Check computers to make sure you can access the simulation.

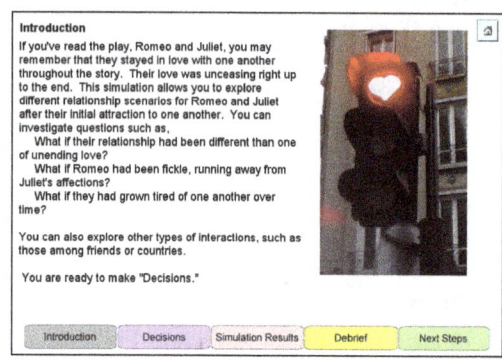

FIGURE 2: Introduction

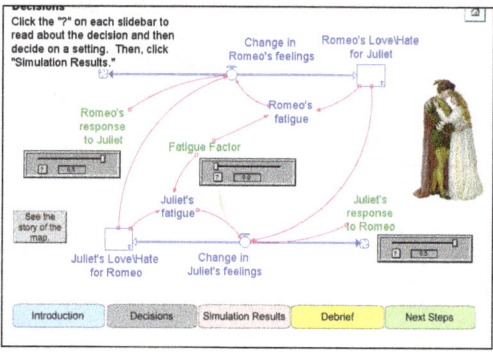

FIGURE 3: Make Decisions

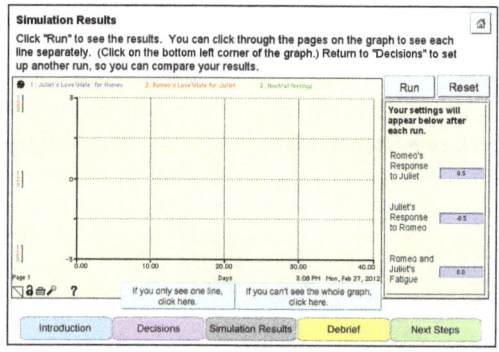

FIGURE 4: Simulation Results

Session 1

1. If the class has read the play, *The Tragedy of Romeo and Juliet*, then use the handout to draw graphs of Juliet's love for Romeo and Romeo's love for Juliet throughout the play (page 4).

2. Have students open the simulation, read the introduction, and view the parts of the simulation on the "Introduction" screen (Figure 2). Note that although the simulation uses the names of Romeo and Juliet, the simulation is not meant to reproduce behavior trends seen within the play. The simulation is a thought experiment that allows students to ask "What if" questions in relation to how the characters in this or other stories might behave. These questions could include, "What if Romeo were fickle, 'playing hard to get' after Juliet indicated interest?" and, "What if the two characters grew tired of one another over time?" Key aspects that students can adjust are:

    a. **Romeo's Response to Juliet** – To what degree does Romeo "play hard to get" if pursued by Juliet? Does he respond wholeheartedly or does he hold back?

    b. **Juliet's Response to Romeo** – To what degree does Juliet "play hard to get" if pursued by Romeo? Does she respond wholeheartedly or does she hold back?

    c. **Romeo and Juliet's fatigue** – To what degree does the couple tire of the relationship?

3. Have students make decisions, run, and then record data on pages 5–9 of the handout as they explore different scenarios and compare the resulting trends (Figures 3 and 4). For the initial exploration runs on page 5 of the handout, you may want to suggest that students change only one variable at a time.

Session 2

1. If needed, have students complete the simulation within their small groups.
2. After students have completed the desired number of simulation runs, they can continue to the "Debrief" section (Figure 5).
3. Debrief the simulation experience using ideas for bringing the lesson home, assessment, and the "Next Steps" section (Figure 6).

Bringing the Lesson Home

- Have students explore the "Debrief" section of the simulation within their small group or as a class.
- Consider why the relationship oscillates, and under what conditions it does not oscillate.
- If students have read the play, *The Tragedy of Romeo and Juliet*, discuss comparisons between the dynamics within the book and those within the simulation.
- Make connections to other systems that oscillate in a similar way. Ideas include, fashion fads, such as skirt length or tie widths, Cold War dynamics (relationship between US and USSR), and friendships.

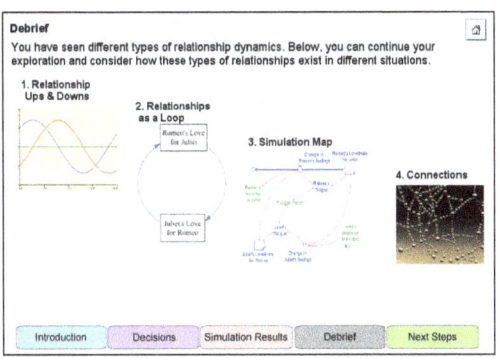

FIGURE 5: Debrief

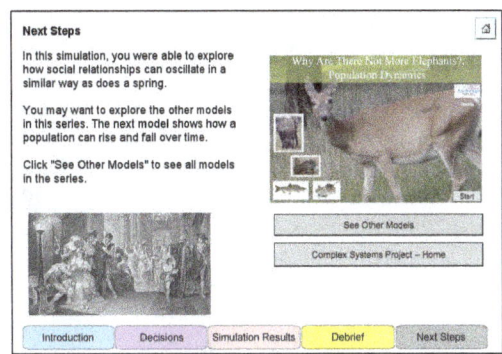

FIGURE 6: Next Steps

Assessment Ideas

- Assessment 1: students tell the story of the relationship dynamics within the map.
- Assessment 2: students identify similar systems.

Note: Assessment Handouts can be formative or summative assessments.

ACKNOWLEDGEMENTS

Lesson 2 – Level B • Romeo and Juliet: Parallel Universe
©2014 Creative Learning Exchange
www.clexchange.org

This model with accompanying lesson is one in a series that explores the characteristics of complex systems.

Model created with contributions from Jen Andersen, Anne LaVigne, Michael Radzicki, George Richardson, Lees Stuntz and with support from Jay Forrester and the Creative Learning Exchange.

Image Credits

Couple snowshoeing, John Boyd, Archives of Ontario, Public Domain.

Friends, by SU09Budi, Wikimedia Commons, Creative Commons Attribution-Share Alike 3.0 Unported (creativecommons.org/licenses/by-sa/3.0/deed.en)

Meeting between President Kennedy and Soviet Foreign Minister Andrei Gromyko, The John F. Kennedy Presidential Library and Museum, Boston. Public Domain.

Heart traffic light, Stuart Mudie, Wikimedia Commons, Creative Commons Attribution - Share Alike 2.0 Generic, (creativecommons.org/licenses/by-sa/2.0/deed.en)

Spider web, US Fish and Wildlife Service, Public Domain.

Dicentra hearts (flowers), Rob Hille, Wikimedia Commons, Public Domain.

Color photolithograph of Romeo/Juliet, Toy Theater print document, Wikimedia Commons, Public Domain.

Engraving of Romeo and Juliet with group, painting by William Miller, engraving by A. Smith, Wikimedia Commons, Public Domain.

Romeo and Juliet by balcony, painting by John Francis Rigaud, engraving by James Stow, Wikimedia Commons, Public Domain.

Hockey players, by Robert Merkel, Wikimedia Commons, Public Domain.

Courtship at Ferry, Edmund Blair Leighton, Art Renewal Center Museum, Public Domain.

Romeo and Juliet Simulation

After reading the play, *The Tragedy of Romeo and Juliet*, graph the levels of love for Romeo toward Juliet and for Juliet toward Romeo over time. Make sure to title your graph, label the y-axis, and create a key for each line on the graph. Note that the zero point on the graph represents "No Love." Anything below zero would be the opposite of love, i.e., hate.

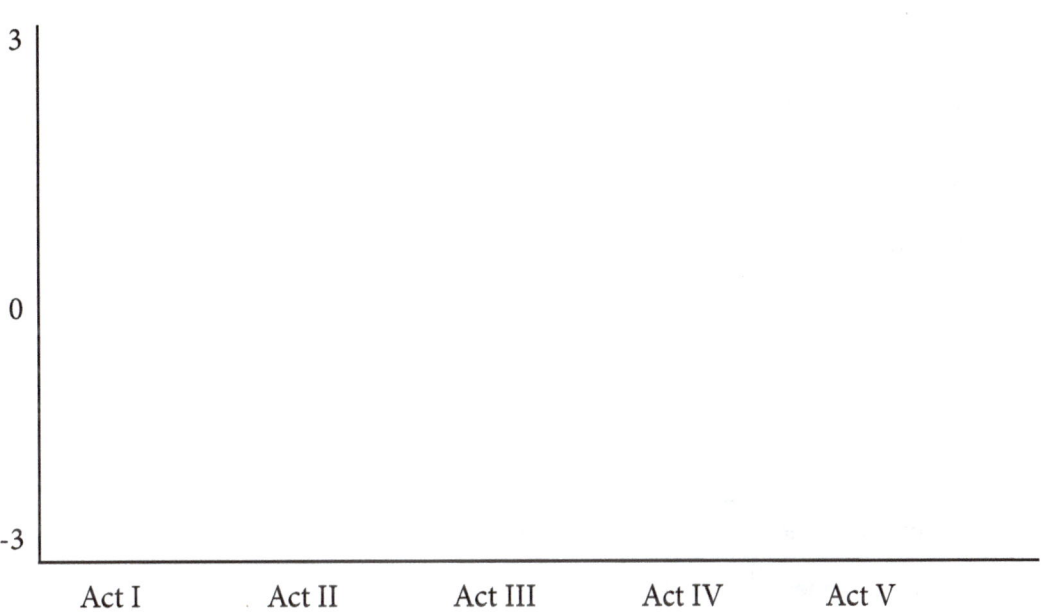

Explain what you think caused these trends to emerge within the story.

_____
_____
_____
_____
_____
_____
_____
_____

Exploring "What If?" Scenarios with Romeo and Juliet

Use the handout and the simulation to create a variety of scenarios, and record your results. For each run, first draw your prediction as a line on the graph, then run and record the actual behaviors. Make sure to create a key to identify the lines on the graph.

Run #_____

Romeo's Response to Juliet	
Juliet's Response to Romeo	
Romeo and Juliet's fatigue	

What happened?

Run #_____

Romeo's Response to Juliet	
Juliet's Response to Romeo	
Romeo and Juliet's fatigue	

What happened?

Run #_____

Romeo's Response to Juliet	
Juliet's Response to Romeo	
Romeo and Juliet's fatigue	

What happened?

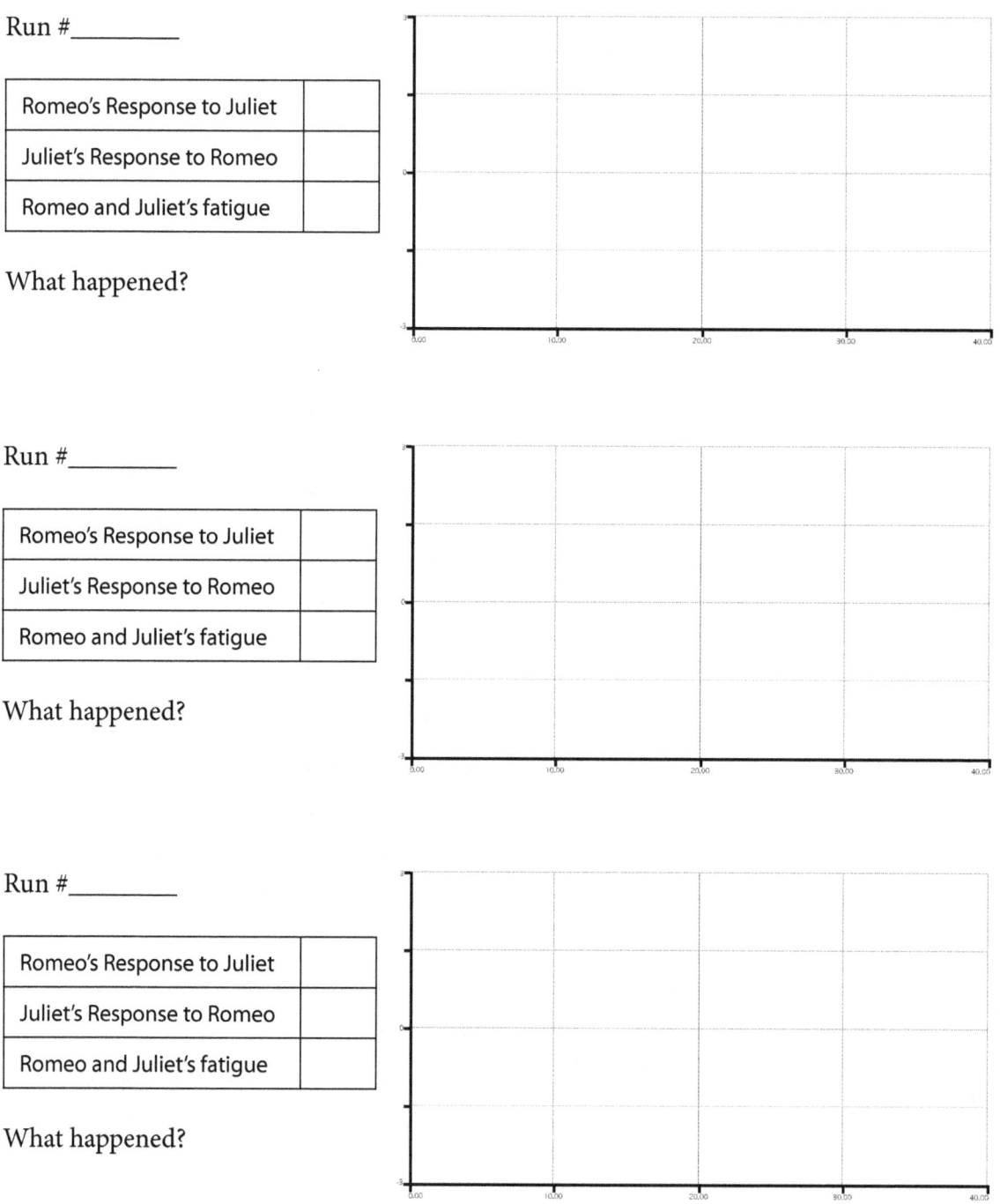

Exploring "What If?" Scenarios with Romeo and Juliet (continued)
Create these specific scenarios and tell the accompanying new stories of Romeo and Juliet's love.

Scenario 1: Romeo and Juliet's love for one another grows over time. The graph should show their love for one another rising throughout the run. Create labels, a key, and a title for the graph.

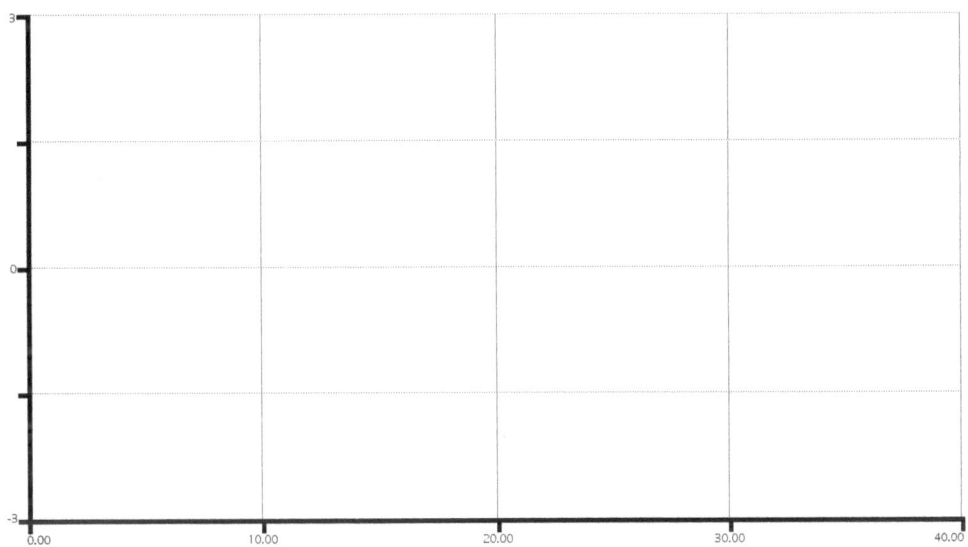

Tell the story of the graph over time.

_____
_____
_____
_____

What conditions did you set to achieve this?

_____
_____
_____
_____
_____
_____

Exploring "What If?" Scenarios with Romeo and Juliet (continued)

Scenario 2: Romeo and Juliet's love oscillates (goes up and down) over time. Sometimes they love one another and sometimes they hate each other. The graph should show their love for one another rising and falling throughout the run. Create labels, a key, and a title for the graph.

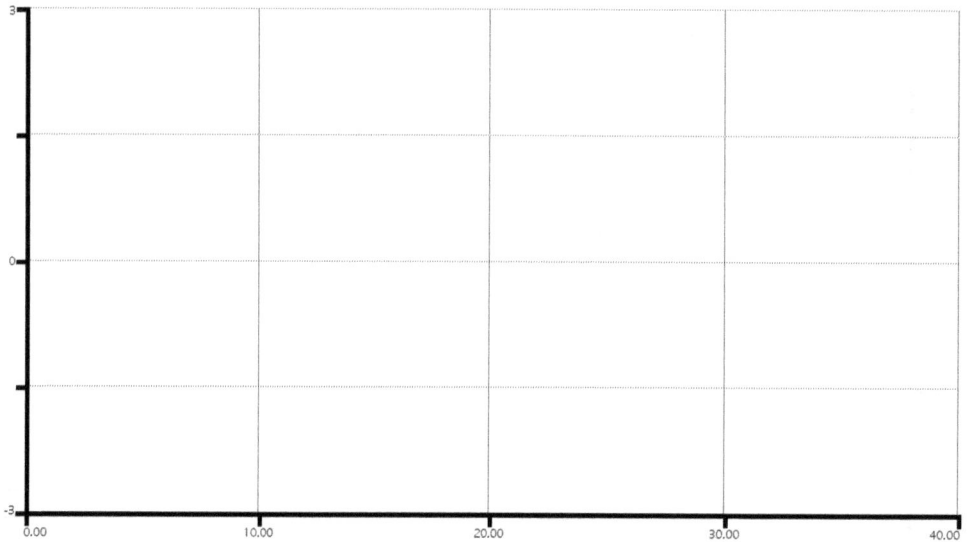

Tell the story of the graph over time.

_____
_____
_____
_____

What conditions did you set to achieve this?

_____
_____
_____
_____
_____

LESSON 2, LEVEL B, HANDOUT – P.5

Exploring "What If?" Scenarios with Romeo and Juliet (continued)

Scenario 3: Romeo and Juliet don't care about each other. The graph should show their love for one another falling throughout the run. Create labels, a key, and a title for the graph.

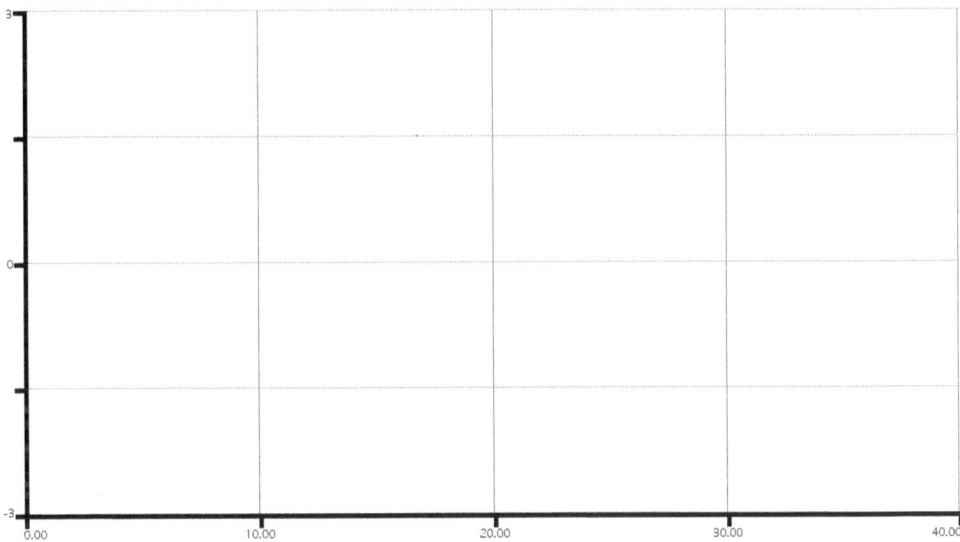

Tell the story of the graph over time.

_____
_____
_____
_____

What conditions did you set to achieve this?

_____
_____
_____
_____
_____
_____

Exploring "What If?" Scenarios with Romeo and Juliet (continued)

Scenario 4: Create your own scenario. Create labels, a key, and a title for the graph.

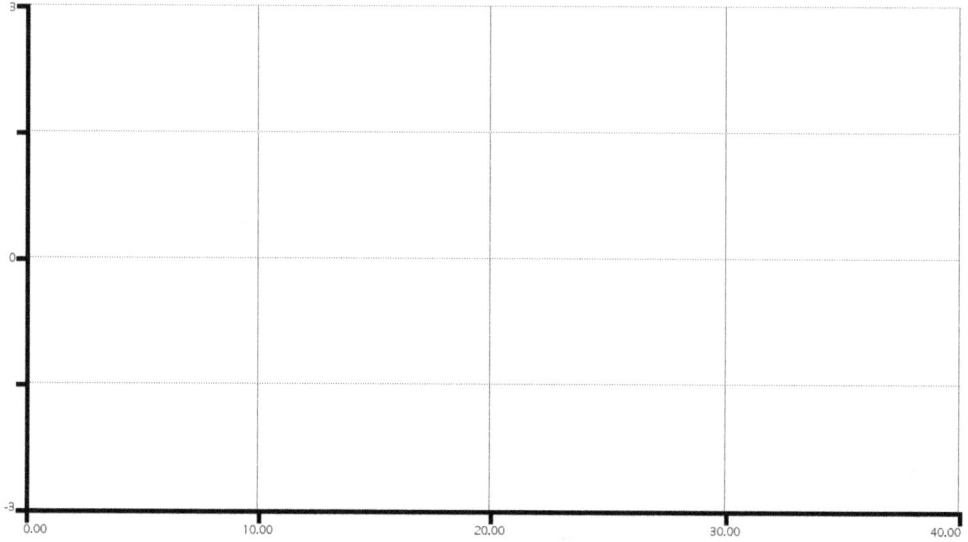

Tell the story of the graph over time.
_____
_____
_____
_____

What conditions did you set to achieve this?
_____
_____
_____
_____
_____

Assessment 1

Look at the map below. Describe the parts and how they impacted Romeo and Juliet's love over time.

Romeo's Response
_____
_____
_____

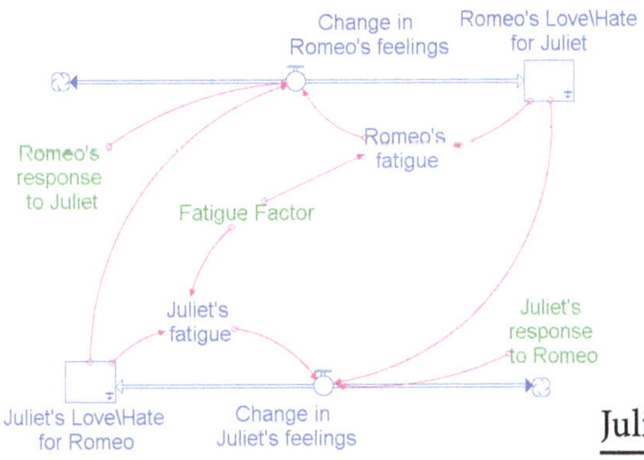

Romeo's Love/Hate
_____
_____
_____

Juliet's Love/Hate
_____
_____
_____

Fatigue Factor:
_____
_____
_____

Juliet's Response:
_____
_____
_____

Tell the story of the relationships within the map. Give examples from the simulation and from real life.

_____
_____
_____
_____
_____
_____
_____
_____
_____
_____

Assessment 2
Draw, title, and label a graph for another situation that behaves in a similar way to Scenario 2, going up and down over time.

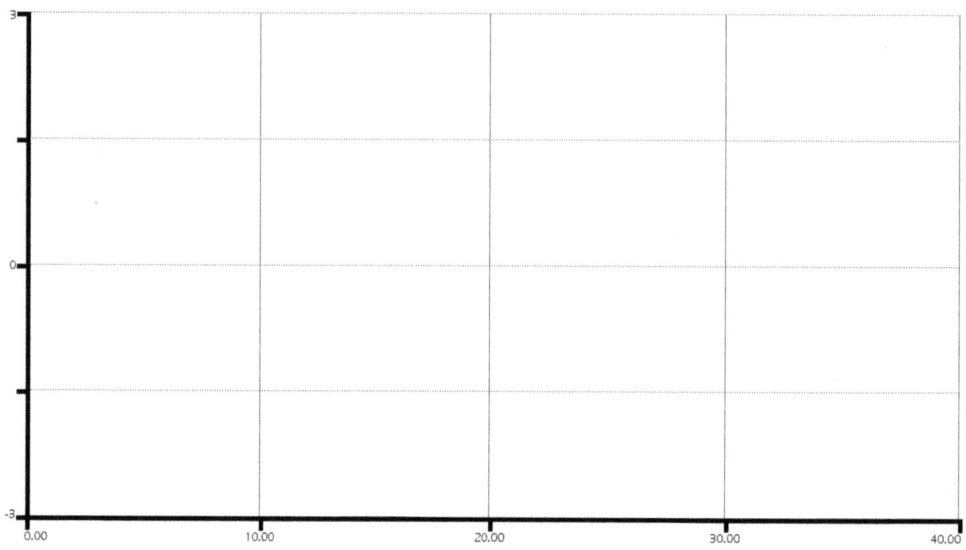

Tell the story of this situation over time.
_____
_____
_____

Use the chart below to create a list of at least three other examples.

Example	Description

Lesson 3 – Level B

Why Are There Not More Elephants? Population Dynamics

Overview

This lesson explores how animal populations can grow and decline over time through use of a simulation (Figure 1). This very simple model allows students to impact the birth and death rates based on input for different animals. The simulation displays what happens to the different populations over time. Students can compare the resulting trends for different animals and consider why those trends occur. Students may also research additional animal data in order to create their own runs.

Learning Goals

- Compare animal population trends through use of a simulation.
- Represent and interpret data on a line graph.
- Describe what impacts an animal population's growth and decline over time.
- Explain why animals are limited in their growth by a carrying capacity.

LESSON 3 – LEVEL B – AGES 8+

Time
Two 45-minute sessions

Materials
- One computer for every 2–3 students
- Handout (See pages 39–44)

Curricular Connections
- Science: Populations, ecosystems, scientific method
- Math: Representing and interpreting data*
- Reading: Describing connections among ideas*

Common Core State Standards

Key system dynamics concepts and insights
- Nature contains limits (carrying capacity) so that populations do not grow forever.
- Populations may grow or decline to carrying capacity.
- Various factors affect how a population grows.

Additional information, based on Level C simulation

FIGURE 1: Title Screen

Student Challenge

Compare animal populations in order to determine which population is most successful over time. Be able to explain why.

Preparation

1. Create groups of 2–3 students each.
2. Copy included handouts for each student or student group. Note: Make multiple copies of page 6, based on the number of simulation runs you would like students to complete. The simulation includes settings for five different animals.
3. Check computers to make sure you can access the simulation.

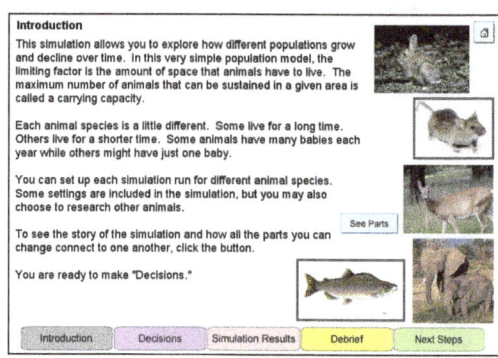

FIGURE 2: Simulation Screen - Introduction

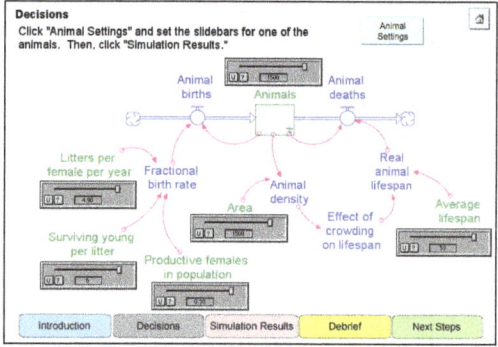

FIGURE 3: Simulation Screen - Decisions

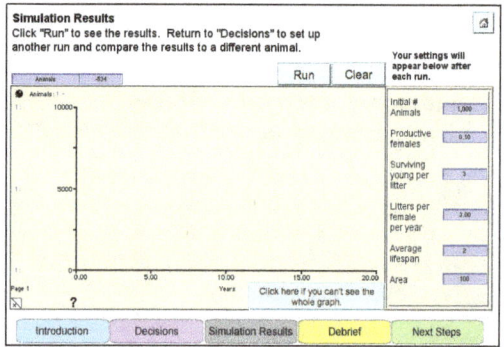

FIGURE 4: Simulation Screen - Simulation Results

Session 1

1. Discuss the following in preparation for using the simulation:

    a. Introduce any vocabulary as needed, including population, lifespan, area, productive female, animal density, birth rate, death rate, and litter size.

    b. Brainstorm a list of animal populations.

    c. How are animal populations similar and different in terms of their reproductive patterns? While students answer the question, ask them to consider average lifespan, litter size, productive females and how these elements interact to help a particular species survive over time. For example, a mouse has many litters and many babies per litter which offsets its short lifespan. An elephant lives a very long time but has very few offspring in comparison to the mouse.

    d. How much space do animals have to live? In the simulation, each of the animals (except the elephant) has 1000 units of land. In reality, different animal populations might have more or less land. For example, a mouse might live on the vacant lot next to a neighborhood or on thousands of acres within a forest.

2. Using page 5 of the handout, have students open the simulation, read the introduction, and view the parts of the simulation on the "Introduction" screen (Figure 2).

3. Students can use page 6 of the handout to record data as they explore different populations and compare the resulting trends (Figures 3 and 4). Note that students will need five or more copies of the handout page, so they can complete multiple simulation runs, making comparisons for different animals.

4. *Additional Options:*

    a. Students can make minor adjustments to the settings for the animals within the simulation, asking questions such as, "What if there were fewer than 1000 animals to begin?" or "What if the animals had more space or less space to live?" Through exploring these questions, they can compare additional trends.

b. Do research on other animals and run the simulation with the new data. Note that not all animals will fit within the confines of the simulation parameters. For example, students would not be able to enter data for an amoeba, since the simulation parameters are not designed to handle the required settings. In addition, if the sliders are pushed to their extremes, the graphs may produce erratic behavior.

5. After they have completed the desired number of simulation runs, students can begin working on the comparison on page 7 of the handout, representing all the animals on one graph.

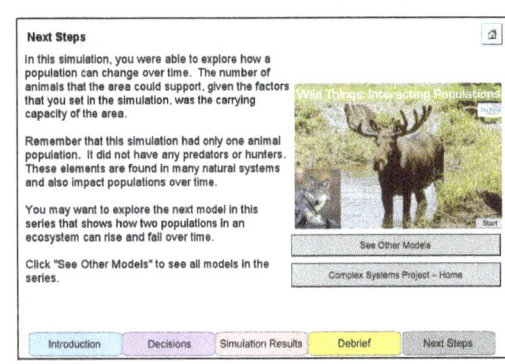

FIGURE 5: Simulation Screen - Debrief

Session 2

1. If needed, have students complete the simulation within their small groups.

2. After running the simulation multiple times, students can continue to the "Debrief" and "Next Steps" sections (Figures 5 and 6).

FIGURE 6: Simulation Screen - Next Steps

3. Debrief the simulation experience using ideas for bringing the lesson home and assessment. For example, after researching an endangered species, collecting information about what impacts both births and deaths, students can complete Assessment 2. See below for an example of a completed map (Figure 7). Note how the student added additional connections (in blue) about their particular

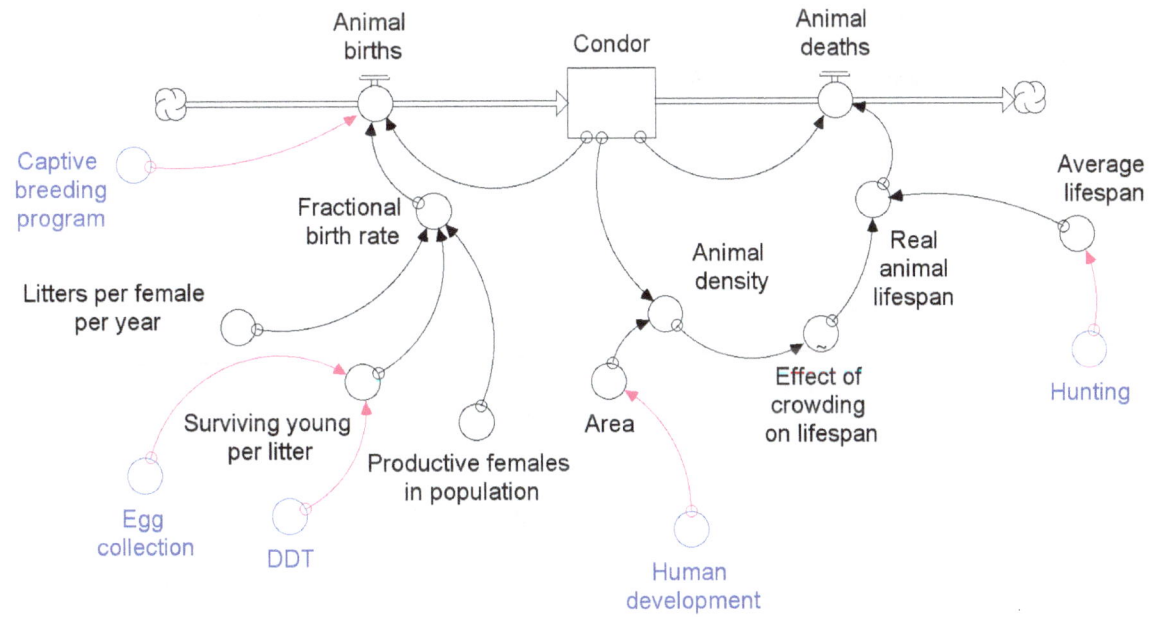

FIGURE 7: Example Completed Debrief Map

Assessment Ideas

Have students use one or more assessments to summarize their learning:

- Assessment 1: to describe the parts of the model and the loops embedded within the simulation.
- Assessment 2: to have students add components to the map to represent an animal they researched.
- Assessment 3: to make connections between the patterns seen in the simulation and other life systems.

animal. They can then "tell the story" of the map, describing the additional elements they included. You might also ask students to include their recommendations for new policies for protecting the species and preventing extinction. The student example shows how a captive breeding program could add to the births.

Bringing the Lesson Home

- Have students explore the "Debrief" section of the simulation within their small group or as a class.
- Consider why the animal population did not grow forever.
- Discuss carrying capacity and how that impacts population growth.

ACKNOWLEDGEMENTS

Lesson 3 – Level B • Why Are There Not More Elephants?: Population Dynamics
©2014 Creative Learning Exchange
www.clexchange.org

This model with accompanying lesson is one in a series that explores the characteristics of complex systems.

Model created with contributions from Jen Andersen, Anne LaVigne, Michael Radzicki, George Richardson, Lees Stuntz, and with support from Jay Forrester and the Creative Learning Exchange.

Image Credits
Salmon - US Fish and Wildlife, Public Domain.
Mouse - NIH.gov, Public Domain.
Rabbit - Anne LaVigne
Deer - by Liscobeck, Wikipedia Project, Public Domain.
Red Wolf and graph - US Fish and Wildlife, Public Domain.
Petri Dish - Ken Hammond, US Dept. of Agriculture, Public Domain.
Elephants - US Fish and Wildlife, Public Domain.
Meadow - Wikimedia Commons, Ace2209, Public Domain.

Elephant with baby - Wikimedia Commons, John Storr, Public Domain.
Hockey players, by Robert Merkel, Wikimedia Commons, Public Domain.
Spider web, US Fish and Wildlife Service, Public Domain.
French Horn, Websters Dictionary, 1911, Wikimedia Commons, Public Domain.
Moose and Wolf - US Fish and Wildlife Service, Public Domain.
Spring - photo by LaVigne.

LESSON 3, LEVEL B, HANDOUT – P.1

Why Are There Not More Elephants Simulation

Click the **Start** button.
Read the **Introduction** screen, View the **See Parts** section, and then answer the following:

What is a carrying capacity? _____
_____

What affects the number of animals in a population? _____
_____

Click **Decisions**.
Read through the information on each of the slidebars by clicking the question marks (**?**). After reading each one, write a definition in your own words below.

Animals: _____
_____

Litters per female per year: _____
_____

Surviving young per litter: _____
_____

Productive females in population: _____
_____

Area: _____
_____

Average lifespan: _____
_____

Click on **Animal Settings** and look at the settings for each of the animals. Which one do you predict will have the largest population after 20 years? Explain why.
_____
_____

Now choose an animal population you would like to explore. Make sure to record all of the information on the simulation record sheet.

Simulation Record Sheet for Run #: ____________________ Animal: ____________________

Initial animals	
Productive females in population	
Litters per female per year	
Surviving young per litter	
Average lifespan	
Area	

What do you think will happen to the population? ____________________

____

What actually happened? Record the final Population #: ____________________
Draw, title and label the y-axis on the graph.

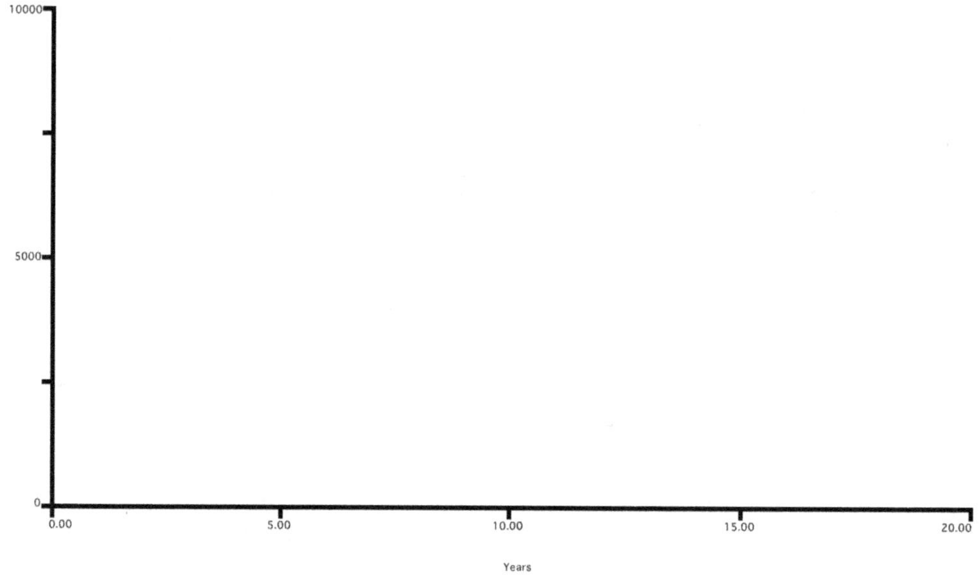

Explain why you think the population changed as it did.

____

____

____

____

____

____

____

Animal Comparisons

Create a key for each of the animals and draw the trends on the graph below.

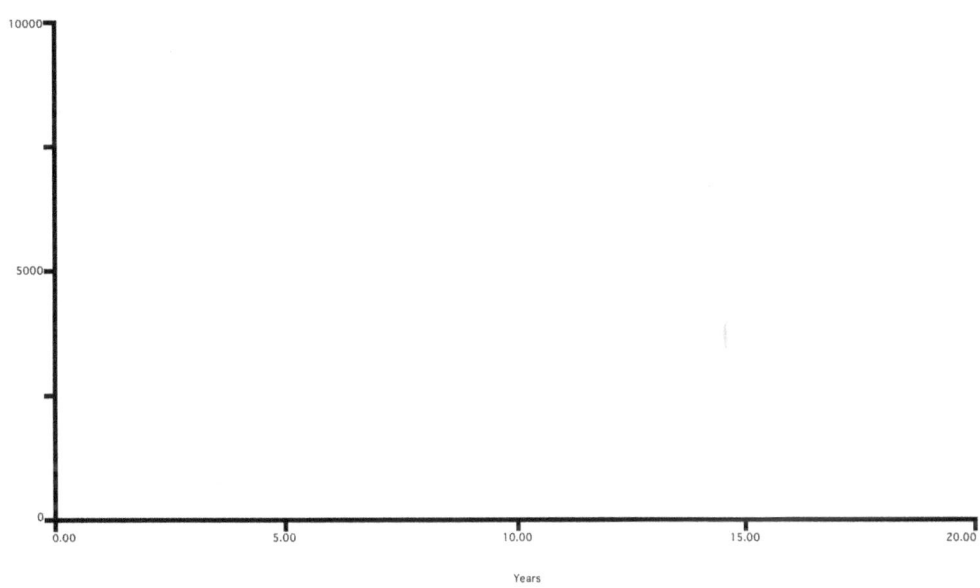

How are the trends similar and different?

_____
_____
_____
_____
_____

Using vocabulary from the simulation, explain why the populations are similar.

_____
_____
_____
_____
_____

Which population grew most quickly? Why?

_____
_____
_____
_____
_____

LESSON 3, LEVEL B, HANDOUT – P.4

Assessment 1
Look at the map below. Describe the parts and how they impacted the population over time.

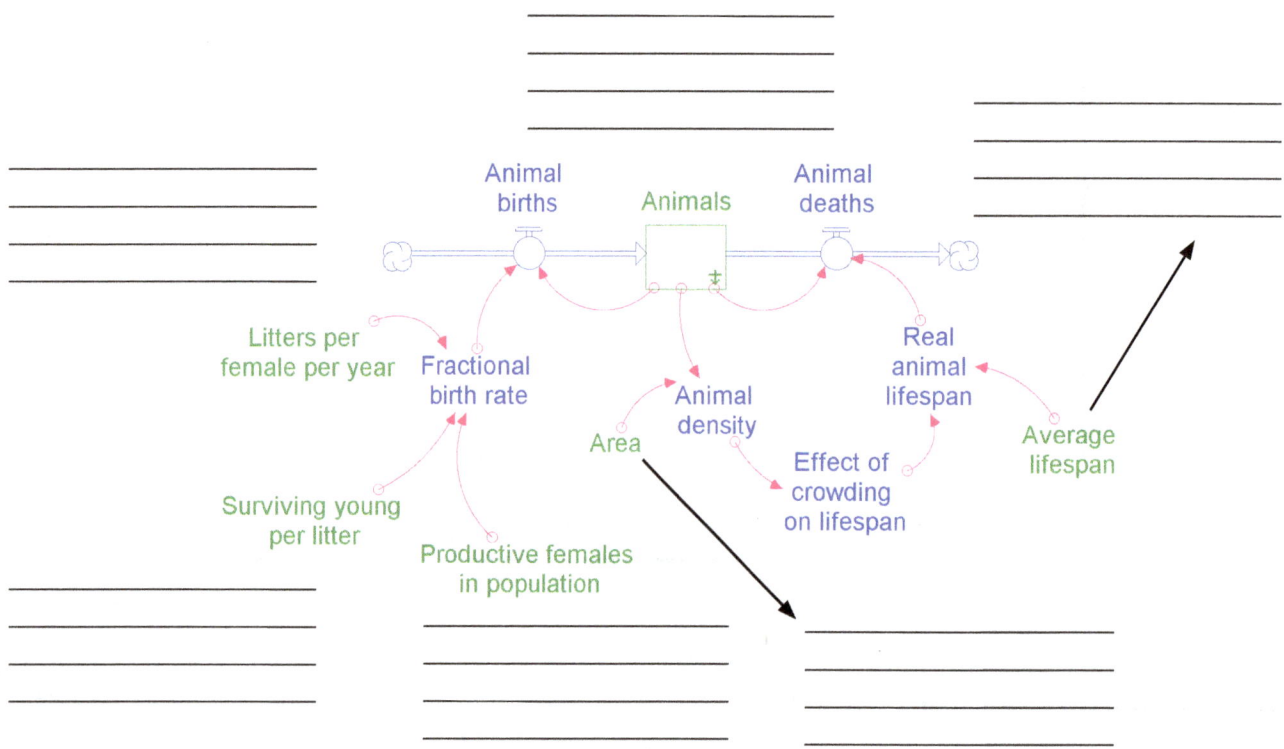

These are two loops within the simulation. Tell the story of each loop in your own words.

42 • LESSON 3 – Level B • Why Are There Not More Elephants? ©2014 Creative Learning Exchange

Assessment 2

Add at least four elements below for an animal that you researched. To add an element, create a circle and add an arrow to show what the element affects. Possible elements could include hunting, poaching, poison within the environment, and conservation efforts. Include an element only if you found evidence to support your connection.

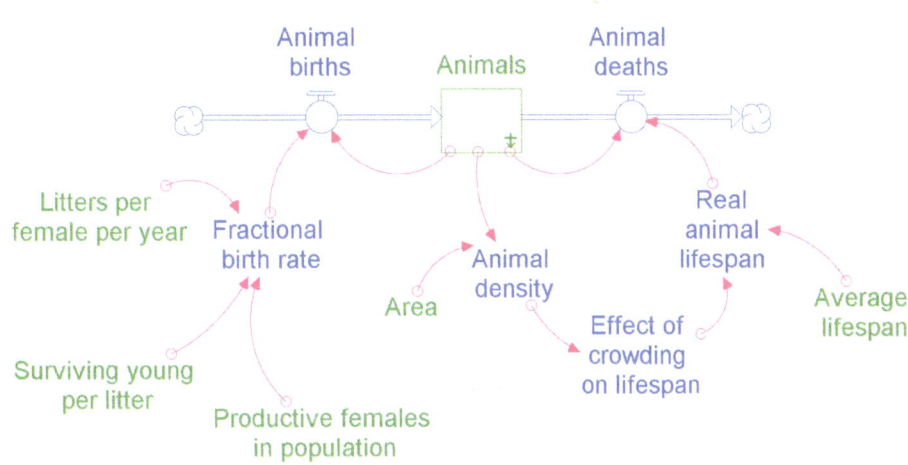

Explain the connections you added.
_____
_____
_____
_____
_____
_____
_____
_____
_____
_____

Assessment 3
Look at the graph, which is similar to many of the animal populations that grew and reached a carrying capacity. What other situations in the world work in a similar manner?

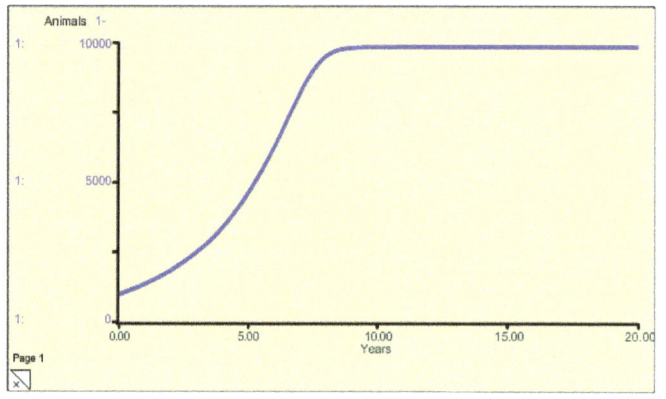

Make a quick list of as many examples as you can.
_____
_____
_____
_____
_____
_____
_____
_____
_____
_____
_____

Choose one of your ideas and tell the story of the graph above, using the example you identified.
_____
_____
_____
_____
_____
_____
_____
_____
_____
_____
_____

Lesson 4 – Level B
Wild Things: Interacting Populations

Overview

This lesson allows students to explore the interactions of two animal populations (predator and prey) within an ecosystem. Their populations can rise and fall (oscillate) over time as they interact and impact one another.

Learning Goals

- Represent and interpret data on a line graph.
- Tell the story of one or more predator/prey feedback loops.
- Create a map showing connections between predator and prey populations.
- Compare results for simulation runs.

LESSON 4 – LEVEL B – AGES 8+

Time
Two or three 45-minute sessions

Materials
- One computer for every 2–3 students
- Handout (See pages 49–56)

Curricular Connections
- Science: Populations, ecosystems, scientific method
- Math: Representing and interpreting data*
- Reading: Describing connections among ideas*

*Common Core State Standards

Key system dynamics concepts and insights
- Models can be used to examine elements affecting births and deaths of two interacting populations.
- Populations do not exist in isolation; other elements (e.g., prey/food supply) affect their growth.
- Predators and their prey form a type of complex system that can exhibit oscillatory behavior.

Additional information, based on Level C simulation

FIGURE 1: Title Screen

Student Challenge

After considering what is causing the two populations to oscillate, create conditions which best stabilize (minimize the oscillations of) the ecosystem on the island.

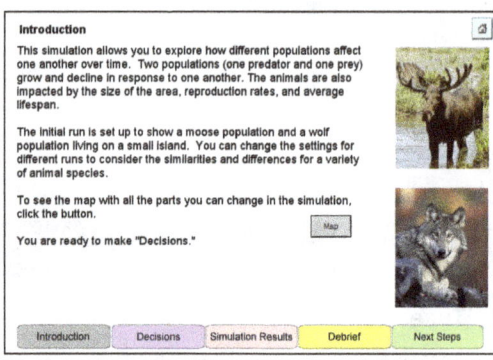

FIGURE 2: Introduction

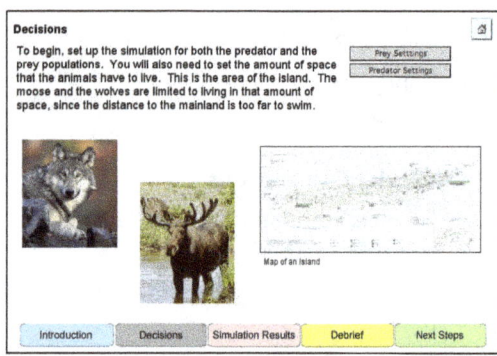

FIGURE 3: Decisions

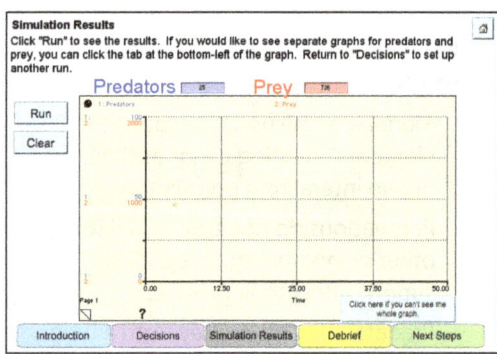

FIGURE 4: Simulation Results

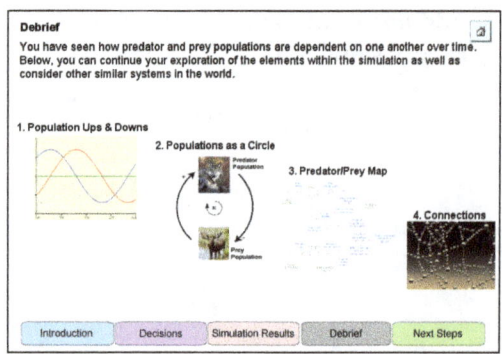

FIGURE 5: Debrief

Lesson Details

Preparation

1. Create groups of 2–3 students each.
2. Copy the handout for each student or student group. Note: Make multiple copies of the handout, based on the number of simulation runs you'd like students to complete. A minimum of three runs is recommended.
3. Check computers to make sure you can access the online simulation.

Session 1

1. Introduce any vocabulary as needed, including population, lifespan, area, density, births factor (rate), deaths factor (rate), predator, and prey.
2. Brainstorm lists of predator and prey animals.
3. Briefly Discuss: What are some physical characteristics of predators? Prey? Do predators rely on just one prey animal? Note: The answer can be yes or no, depending on the environment. In the initial case study of the moose/wolf populations, the answer is mostly yes, since moose is the main prey animal available on the island ecosystem.
4. Have students open the simulation, read the introduction, and view the parts of the simulation on the "Introduction" screen. (Figure 2)
5. Students can now set up the simulation for the moose and wolf populations on the "Decisions" screens. (Figure 3)
6. Have students record data on the handouts as they explore predator and prey populations and describe the resulting trends. (Figure 4)
7. Additional options for student exploration include:
   a. Option #1: Ask and test a variety of "What if" questions relating to the moose and wolf populations. See handout on page 7.
   b. Option #2: Research additional animals and create a comparison for different predator/prey populations.

Session 2

1. If needed, have students complete the simulation within their small groups.
2. After running the simulation multiple times, students can continue to the "Debrief" section. (Figure 5)

3. Debrief the simulation experience using ideas for bringing the lesson home and assessment options. Examples (Figures 6 and 7) show possible student responses on both the debrief and assessments handouts. Below are stories to accompany those graphic representations.
4. Story of the example map in Figure 6: The wolves affect the prey by eating them. The moose population goes down because wolves kill them, people hunt them, and they die of natural causes. The moose also affect the wolves because having enough to eat helps them stay healthy, live long lives and have more babies. If there are not enough moose, the wolves can starve to death.
5. Below are examples stories for loops shown in Figure 7. Note: To write these stories, students can start with any stock and decide, "Is it going up or going down?" From there, the student can trace along the direction of the arrows, explaining the causes and effects all the way around until back to the point of origin.

Bringing the Lesson Home

- Have students explore the "Debrief" and "Next Steps" sections of the simulation within their small group or as a class.
- Discuss the trends on the graphs. What caused the population to oscillate? How did hunting impact the oscillations? If you were a hunter who relied on hunting to feed your family, how might population levels affect your success?

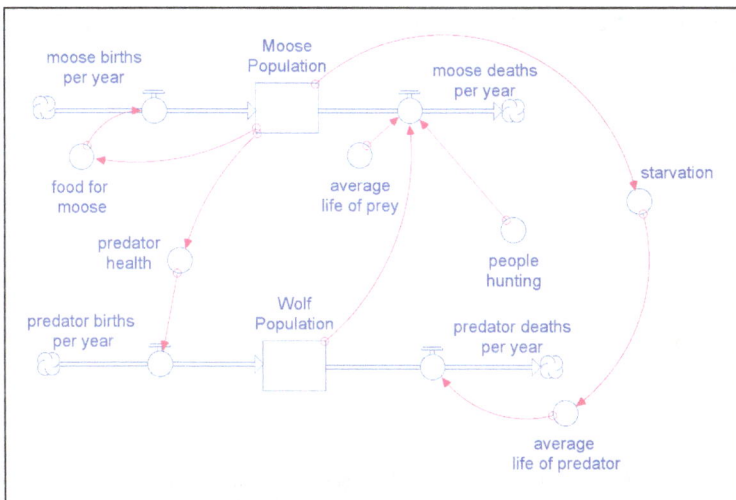

Assessment Ideas

Have students use one or more of the assessment handouts:

- "Debrief" handout allows students to tell the story of a feedback loop and create connections on a predator/prey stock/flow map for either the moose/wolf populations or another animal they researched.
- "Assessment" handout allows students to find feedback loops within the full simulation map and to tell the story of the map/loops.

FIGURE 6: Example Completed Stock/Flow Map

Loop Stories for Diagram in Figure 7

Loop 1 Story

- If the prey population rises, the density will rise. This will create a big effect on the prey lifespan because they'll be more crowded.
- As the effect gets bigger, the lifespan for prey will drop, causing a greater number of prey deaths and fewer prey in the stock.

Loop 2 Story

If the prey population rises, the density will rise. This will create an effect, since the prey would be easier to find. As the effect gets bigger, more prey will be killed by each predator. This will cause more prey to die (outflow), thus causing a decrease in the number of prey in the stock.

Loop 3 Story

As the predator population rises, the prey killed will increase, causing the prey population to decrease. As there are fewer prey, the prey density will go down. This will create an effect, since the prey would be harder to find. As the effect gets bigger, it creates another effect on the predator lifespan. Since the predators have less to eat, they will not live as long. As their lifespan goes down, predator deaths will go up, causing there to be fewer predators. Notice that the predator population first went up at the beginning of the story and went down at the end. If we go around the loop again, it will go back up again.

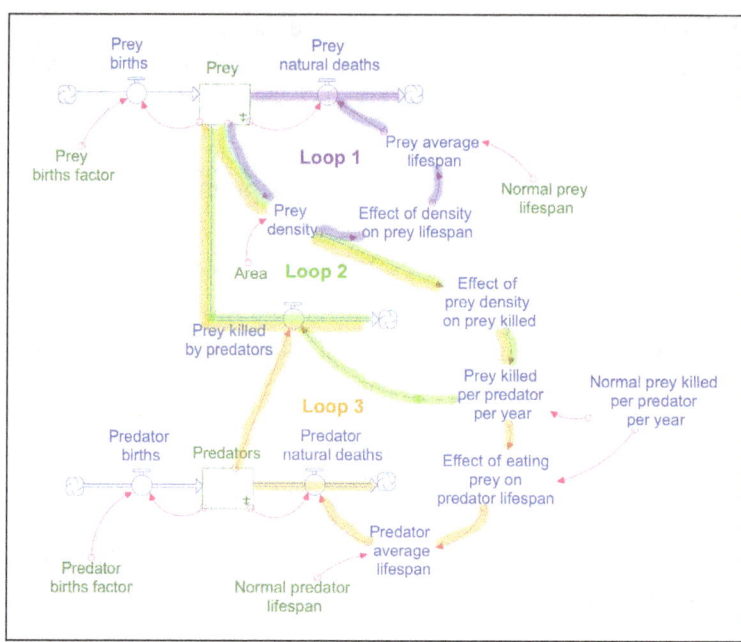

FIGURE 7: Example Loops for Page 9 Assessment

ACKNOWLEDGEMENTS

Lesson 4 – Level B • Wild Things: Interacting Populations
©2014 Creative Learning Exchange
www.clexchange.org

This model with accompanying lesson is one in a series that explores the characteristics of complex systems.

Model created with contributions from Jen Andersen, Anne LaVigne, Michael Radzicki, George Richardson, Lees Stuntz, and with support from Jay Forrester and the Creative Learning Exchange.

Image Credits

Moose and wolf - US Fish and Wildlife Service, Public Domain.
Boy with toys, Wikimedia Commons, Nationaal Archief/Spaarnestad Photo/ W.P. van de Hoef, Public Domain.
Girl eating, Wikimedia Commons, Renoir, Public Domain.
Hand holding spring, LaVigne, photo used with Permission.
Spider web, U.S. Fish and Wildlife Service, Public Domain.
Map of Isle Royale, National Park Service, Public Domain.

LESSON 4, LEVEL B, HANDOUT – P.1

Interacting Populations Simulation

Click the **Start** button.
Read the **Introduction** screen, View the **Map, See the story of the full map,** and then answer the following:

What do the predators need to survive? _____
_____

What elements are present in the real world that would also impact the prey population?
_____
_____

Click **Decisions.**
Click **Prey Settings.** Read through the information on each of the slidebars by clicking the question marks (**?**). After reading each one, write a definition in your own words below.

Prey _____
_____

Prey births factor _____
_____

Normal prey lifespan _____
_____

Area _____
_____

Click **Predator Settings** and do the same as above.

Predators _____
_____

Predator births factor _____
_____

Normal prey lifespan _____
_____

©2014 Creative Learning Exchange   LESSON 4 – Level B • Interacting Populations • 49

Baseline Run

Input the values shown below onto the simulation screen, but don't run it just yet.

Predator	Wolf
Initial predators	20
Births factor	0.3
Normal lifespan	8 years
Area	200 square miles

Prey	Moose
Initial prey	800
Births factor	0.4
Normal lifespan	12 years

What do you predict will happen to the two populations?
_____
_____

Click **Run.** Now record your results below. Using two colors, you need to:

1. Create a key.
2. Title your graph.
3. Write in the scales on the y-axis.
4. Draw the graph lines for the two populations.

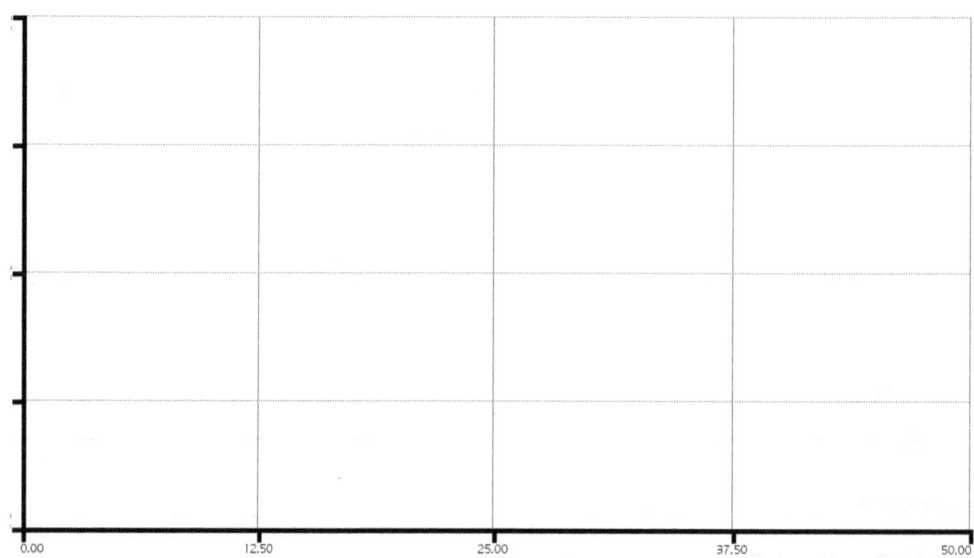

Interacting Populations Simulation

Explain why you think the populations changed as they did.

_____
_____
_____
_____
_____
_____
_____

Continue your exploration, asking "What if" questions. Try ideas one at a time and then record what happens on a new sheet.

Question 1: What might happen if the animals had less space to live?

Question 2: What might happen if the animals had more space to live?

Question 3: What might happen if the island had more wolves to start?

Question 4: What settings create the most stable populations (not too many ups and downs)?

Question 5: What are some other questions you could explore? Write one or more questions below and try them one at a time.

_____
_____
_____
_____
_____
_____
_____

LESSON 4, LEVEL B, HANDOUT – P.4

Experimental Runs

Run #: _____   Question: _____

Predator	
Initial predators	
Births factor	
Normal lifespan	
Area	

Prey	
Initial prey	
Births factor	
Normal lifespan	

What do you think will happen to the two populations?
_____
_____

Click **Run**. Now record your results below. Using two colors, you need to:

1. Create a key.
2. Title your graph.
3. Write in the scales on the y-axis.
4. Draw the graph lines for the two populations.

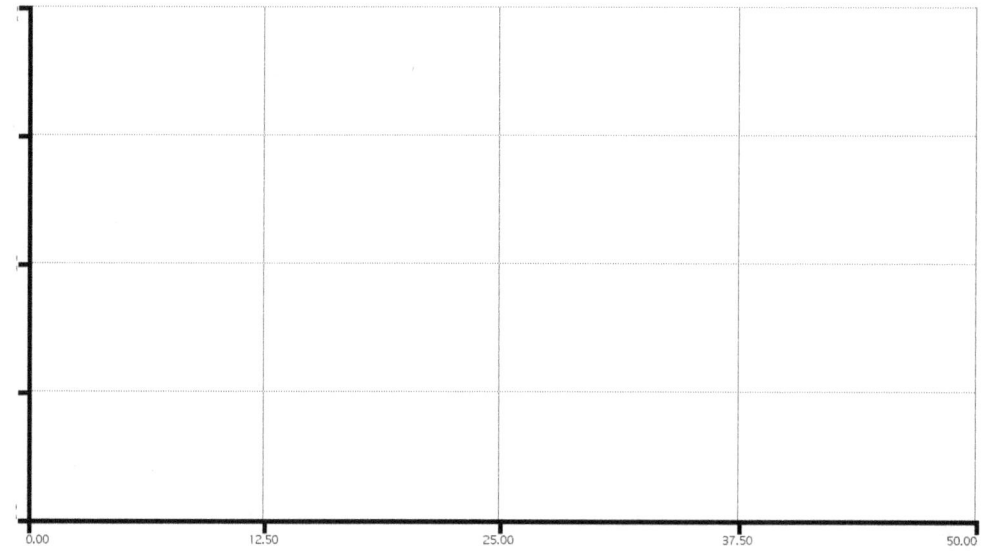

52 • LESSON 4 – Level B • Interacting Populations   ©2014 Creative Learning Exchange

LESSON 4, LEVEL B, HANDOUT – P.5

Run Analysis

1. How does this run compare to the baseline run? What's similar? What's different?
___
___
___
___
___
___

2. What is causing the similarities and differences?
___
___
___
___

3. Why do you think the populations changed as they did?
___
___
___
___

4. How do the numbers of moose and wolves affect one another? You can draw your ideas if you'd like.

Debrief

Go back to the Menu and click, **Debrief**. Explore each of the four sections, answering the questions below after completing each one.

Click 1. Population Ups and Downs.
a. What is the term used to describe a graph that goes up and down over time?
_____

b. How do the predator and prey populations affect one another? Use the graph to help you.
_____
_____
_____

Click 2. Populations as a Circle.
a. Why does the loop of predator and prey balance over time?
_____
_____
_____

Click 3. Predator/Prey Map.
a. Use this map to describe the relationships between predator and prey.

b. Draw a map below for one predator/prey relationship, either the moose/wolf populations or another animal that you researched. To add an element, create a circle and add an arrow to show what the element affects. Possible elements could include hunting, poaching, lifespan, and birth factor. Include an element only if you found evidence to support your connection. On a separate piece of paper, tell the story of your map.

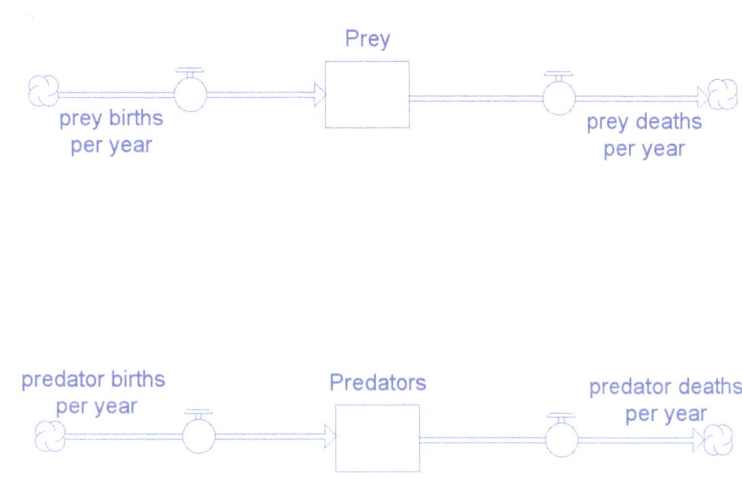

c. Why do you think having a lot of prey is good for the predators but bad for the prey?

Click **4. Connections.**
a. What are some other connections you can see between predator/prey relationships and other systems in the world?

Assessment

Describe the story of the map. Make sure to describe at least one loop.

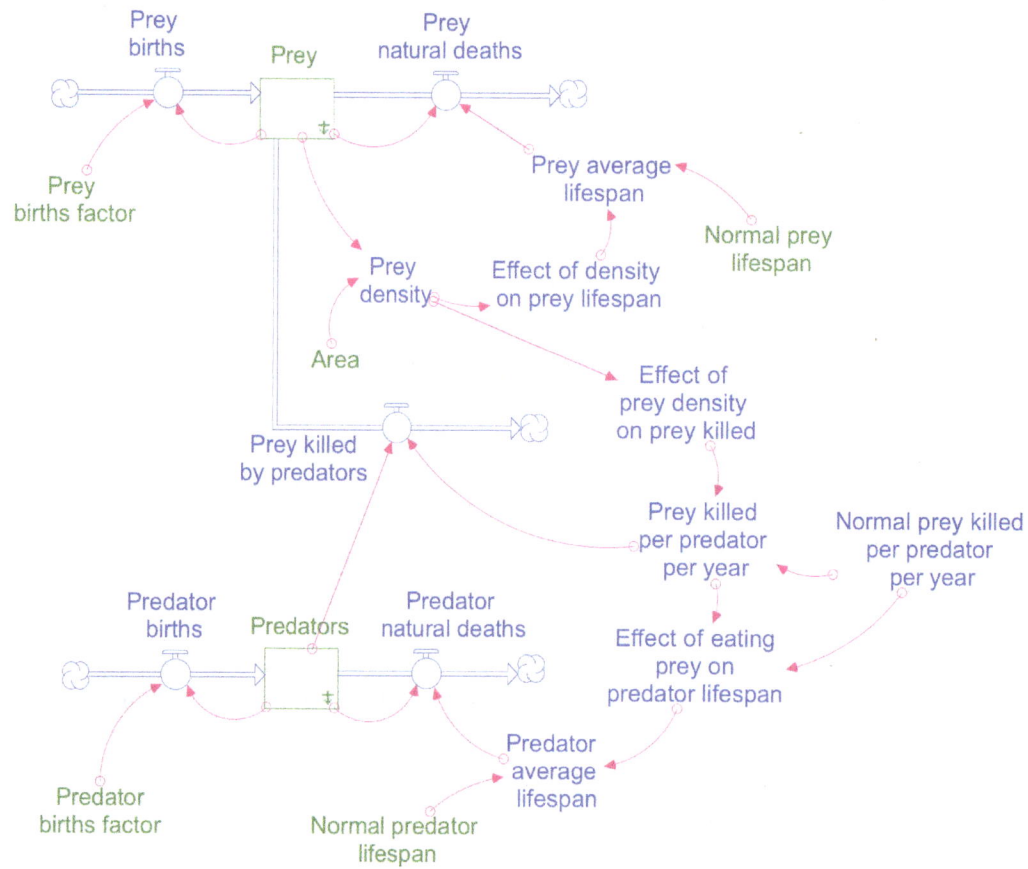

Lesson 5 – Level B

Circles of Interaction: Predator, Prey, and Plants

Overview

This lesson explores predator (wolf), prey (moose), and food (plants) within an ecosystem. Students role-play being a wildlife manager who is doing "on the job" training. The manager controls hunting of prey populations and killing of predators. The default simulation behavior for prey, predators, and food is oscillation.

Learning Goals

- Represent and interpret data on a line graph.
- Compare results for simulation runs.
- Manage a simulated ecosystem, keeping it healthy.
- Identify and explain challenges of being a wildlife manager and meeting specific goals.

FIGURE 1: Title Screen

Student Challenge

Keep the ecosystem healthy while managing related human interests, even in the face of unexpected events, such as a drought.

LESSON 5 – LEVEL B – AGES 8+

Time
Three or more 45-minute sessions

Materials
- One computer for every 2-3 students
- Handouts (See pages 60–74)

Curricular Connections
- Science: Populations, ecosystems, scientific method
- Math: Representing and interpreting data*
- Reading: Describing connections among ideas*

*Common Core State Standards

Key system dynamics concepts and insights
- Models can be used to examine elements affecting births and deaths of two interacting populations.
- Populations do not exist in isolation; other elements (e.g., prey/food supply) affect their growth.
- Predators and their prey form a type of complex system that can exhibit oscillatory behavior.

Additional information, based on Level C simulation

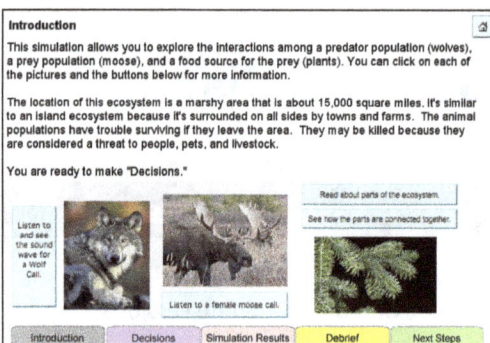

FIGURE 2: Introduction

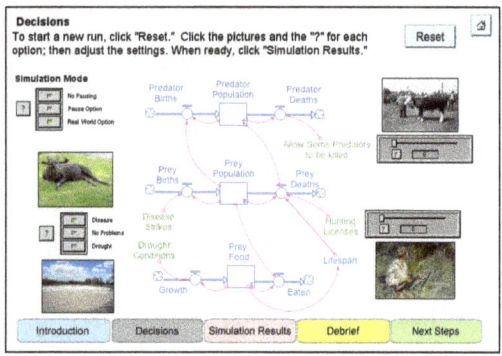

FIGURE 3: Decisions

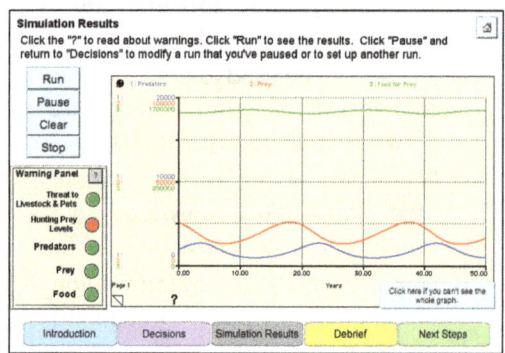

FIGURE 4: Simulation Results

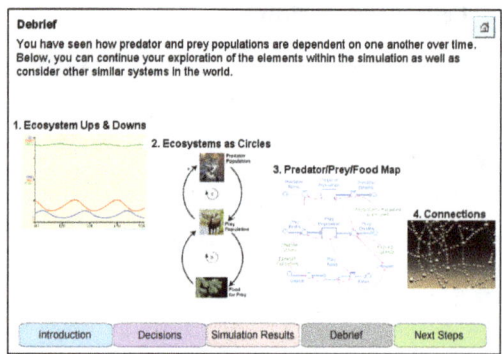

FIGURE 5: Debrief

Lesson Details

Preparation

1. Create groups of 2–3 students each.
2. Copy all handouts for each student or student group.
3. Check computers to make sure you can access the online simulation.

Session 1

1. Introduce any vocabulary as needed, including population, predator, prey, food (in the form of plants for the prey), herbivore, carnivore, omnivore, hunting license.
2. Brainstorm lists of predators, their prey, and prey food sources. Discuss the different diets of animals along with the associated labels. This simulation focuses on a wolf population that has the main diet of moose. The moose mainly eats grasses and the new growth from local trees, such as the balsam fir.
3. Describe the final project in which students put together a final report to their "boss." Go over the requirements and rubric. (Handout 1, page 60)
4. Have students open the simulation and read the introduction. (Handout 1 and Figure 2).
5. Students can now set up the simulation for the moose and wolf populations on the "Decisions" screens (Figure 3). As they do this, have students record data as they work through the experiments and challenges in the handouts (Handout 2, page 62 and Figure 4).

Session 2

1. If needed, have students complete the simulation within their small groups.
2. After working through the challenges, students can continue to the "Debrief" section (Handout 3, page 69, and Figure 5).
3. Debrief the simulation experience using ideas for bringing the lesson home and generating assessment ideas. The important work of this lesson is a write-up that summarizes the learning and makes a policy proposal based on those findings (Handout 4, page 71).
4. A second, optional assessment allows students to show their understanding of the interconnections among the

main simulation elements (Handout 5, page 74). See below for one possible "story" of the loops.

Example Story: The wolves eat moose. If the wolf population goes up, then the moose population will likely go down. The moose population also affects the wolves, because having enough to eat helps them stay healthy, live long lives and have more babies. If the moose population goes down, the wolf population will likely also go down. Also, the food available for moose changes what happens. If the moose population goes up, then the amount of food will likely go down. If the food supply goes down, the moose population will probably be reduced, due to starvation.

Bringing the Lesson Home

- Have students explore the "Debrief" and "Next Steps" sections of the simulation within their small group or as a class (Handout 3, page 69).
- Discuss the trends on the graphs. What caused the population to oscillate? How did hunting impact the oscillations? If you were a hunter who relied on hunting to feed your family, how might population levels affect your success?

Assessment Ideas

- Create a write-up of findings in a report to the Park Director (Handout 4, pages 71–73).
- Describe the interactions among the main simulation elements (Handout 5, page 74).

ACKNOWLEDGEMENTS

Lesson 5 – Level B • Circles of Interaction: Predator, Prey, and Plants ©2014 Creative Learning Exchange

This model is one in a series of models that explores the characteristics of complex systems.

Model created with contributions from Jen Andersen, Anne LaVigne, Michael Radzicki, George Richardson, Lees Stuntz, and with support from Jay Forrester and the Creative Learning Exchange.

Image Credits
Wolf, Gary Kramer, USFWS, Public Domain.
Balsam Fir, USDA, Public Domain.
Moose (title page), USFWS, Public Domain.
Moose (intro page), USFWS, Public Domain.
Wolf call, USFWS, Public Domain.
Sound wave, USFWS, Public Domain.
Moose call, USFWS, Public Domain.
Trophic pyramid, by Thompsma, Wikimedia Commons, Creative Commons Attribution -ShareAlike 3.0 Unported license (http://creativecommons.org/licenses/by-sa/3.0/deed.en).
Moose reclining, by Zaereth, Wikimedia Commons, Public Domain.

Hunter painting, Bruno Liljefors, Public Domain.
Boy with cow, ca.1923, Public Domain.
Dry riverbed, Kirk Miller, USGS, US Dept. of the Interior, Public Domain.
Spider web, USFWS, Public Domain.
Spring, Photo by A.LaVigne, Used with Permission.
City scene, Detroit Publishing Company, ca.1900, Public Domain.
Gas price sign, Dorothea Lange, US Farm Security Administration, Public Domain.
Gas price graph, US Dept of Energy, Public Domain.

LESSON 5, LEVEL B, HANDOUT 1 – P.1

Predator, Prey, and Plants – Introduction

You just started a new job working in a national park. As part of your on-the-job training, you will run a simulation. You will decide how much moose hunting is allowed. You will also decide if it's OK for people to kill wolves. This will help you write a report to your boss, Rutheforest T. Grove, about what you've learned.

The report should include:
1. Title page
   - Title: Ecosystem Report
   - Name and Date
   - A picture of the ecosystem, including each part. You can create a collage, drawing, or other representation to show the parts of the ecosystem and how they are connected.
2. Your report to the Park Director, Rutheforest T. Grove. Before you begin writing your report, you need to copy your graphs from Handout 2. Then use those graphs to explain your plan to the Park Director.
3. Handouts 1–4, complete and organized neatly in order
   - Handout 1 – Instructions, Rubric, and Introduction
   - Handout 2 – Baseline and Challenge Runs
   - Handout 3 – Debrief
   - Handout 4 – Report to the Park Director

Project Assessment Rubric

	Novice	Basic	Proficient	Advanced
Title Page	My pictures are not about the ecosystem.	I have pictures, but I didn't show any connections.	My pictures have important parts of the ecosystem and show how they are connected.	In addition, I have added words to explain the connections.
Handouts	I didn't explain what happened.	I recorded results that were mostly accurate. I explained what happened.	I recorded results that were accurate. I clearly explained what happened and why.	In addition, I am able to meet each challenge and can explain why I was successful.
My Report to the Park Director	My report is missing, or very little is included to show my learning.	I wrote a summary of my learning, but I did not include proof from the simulation.	I wrote a clear summary of my learning, using proof from the simulation.	In addition, I can explain my learning as a recommended plan to the Park Director.

LESSON 5, LEVEL B, HANDOUT 1 – P.2

Click the **Start** button.
Read the **Introduction** screen, click on the pictures and listen to the sounds.

What do the prey need to survive? _____
_____

What is one issue relating to the predators? _____
_____
_____

Why do you think that this area is being called an "island ecosystem" even though it's not surrounded by water? _____
_____

Click "Read about parts of the simulation." Read and then **click** on each of the levels.

On what level is the moose in our simulation? _____

On what level is the wolf in our simulation? _____

What does the moose eat? _____

Click "Decisions." Read through the information by clicking the question marks (**?**) for each of the decisions. After reading each one, write a definition in your own words below.

Simulation Mode _____
_____

Disease _____
_____

Drought _____
_____

Allow some predators to be killed _____
_____

Hunting licenses _____
_____

©2014 Creative Learning Exchange

LESSON 5, LEVEL B, HANDOUT 2 – P.1

Predator, Prey and Plants – Baseline Run and Exploration

Set up the simulation as shown below, but don't run it just yet.

Simulation Mode	No Pausing and No Problems
Prey hunting (licenses)	0
Predator hunting	0

What do you predict will happen to the two populations and the food?
_____
_____
_____

At the bottom of the screen, go to **Simulation Results,** and **Click "Run."** Now record your results below. Using three colors, you need to:
1. Create a key.
2. Title your graph.
4. Draw the graph lines for the populations and the food.

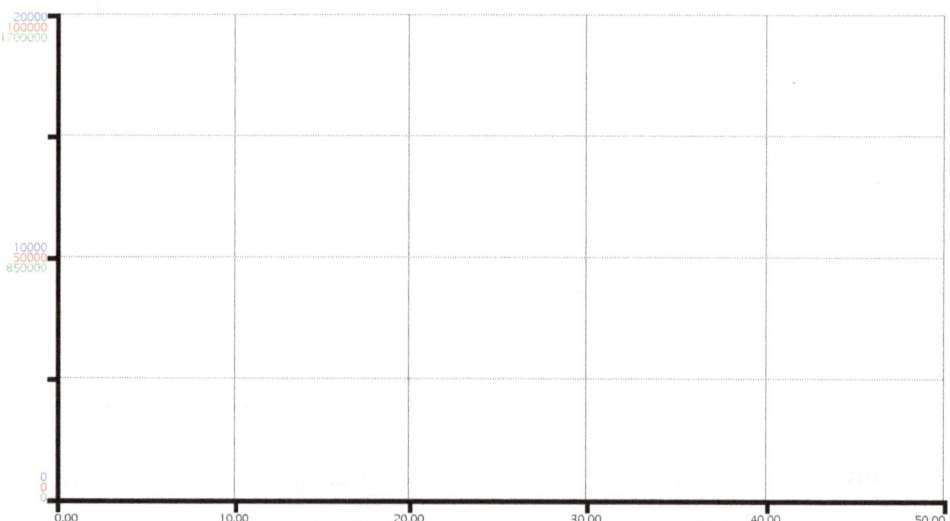

62 • LESSON 5 – Level B • Predator, Prey, and Plants ©2014 Creative Learning Exchange

LESSON 5, LEVEL B, HANDOUT 2 – P.3

Explain what happened and why.

_____
_____
_____
_____
_____

Continue your exploration, asking "What if" questions. Try ideas one at a time.

Question 1: What might happen if I allow some hunting of prey?
Question 2: What might happen if I allow some predators to be killed?
Question 3: What might happen if I allow both prey hunting and predator kills?
Question 4: What might happen if I allow a very high level of hunting either predators or prey or both?

What have you learned so far?

_____
_____
_____
_____
_____
_____
_____
_____
_____
_____
_____
_____
_____
_____
_____
_____
_____
_____
_____
_____

Challenge #1: Can you keep the ecosystem healthy?

Return to **Decisions** and set the simulation mode to "Pausing."
Go to **Simulation Results**, run the simulation and make changes as needed every time the simulation pauses. Record your settings in the table as you go.

Year	Prey hunting (licenses)	Predator hunting
0		
10		
20		
30		
40		

Record your results on the graph as before.

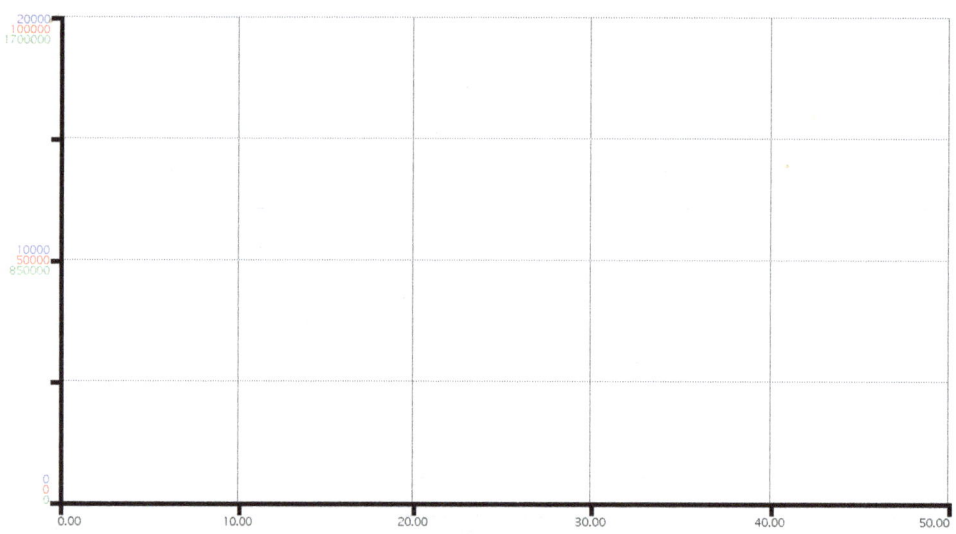

a. Explain what happened and why.

_____
_____
_____
_____
_____
_____

b. Were you able to keep the graphs mostly flat like this?
_____

Why or why not?
_____
_____

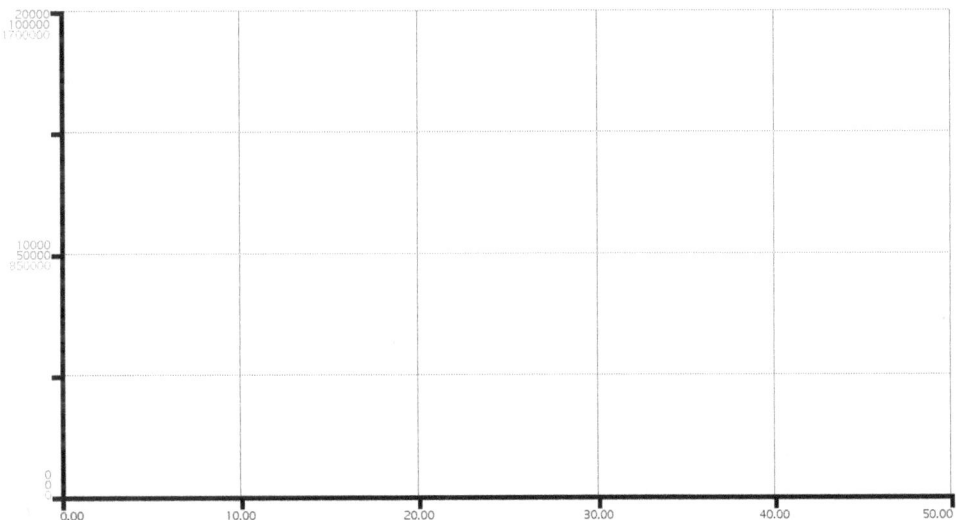

Graph of a Healthy, Stable Ecosystem

c. What could you do differently?
_____
_____
_____
_____

Continue running the simulation in pause mode, trying different plans. Record the graph for your best run below.

d. What worked best and why?
_____
_____
_____
_____
_____

LESSON 5, LEVEL B, HANDOUT 2 – P.5

Challenge #2: Can you keep the ecosystem in balance, while meeting the needs of the hunters, residents, and farmers?

On the **Decisions** page, set the simulation mode to "Real world."
Run the simulation and make changes as needed. You can pause whenever you like to make changes. Record the year (top of graph), messages, and any changes to your settings below.

Year	Message Issue	Prey hunting (licenses)	Predator hunting
0	None		

Record your results on the graph as before.

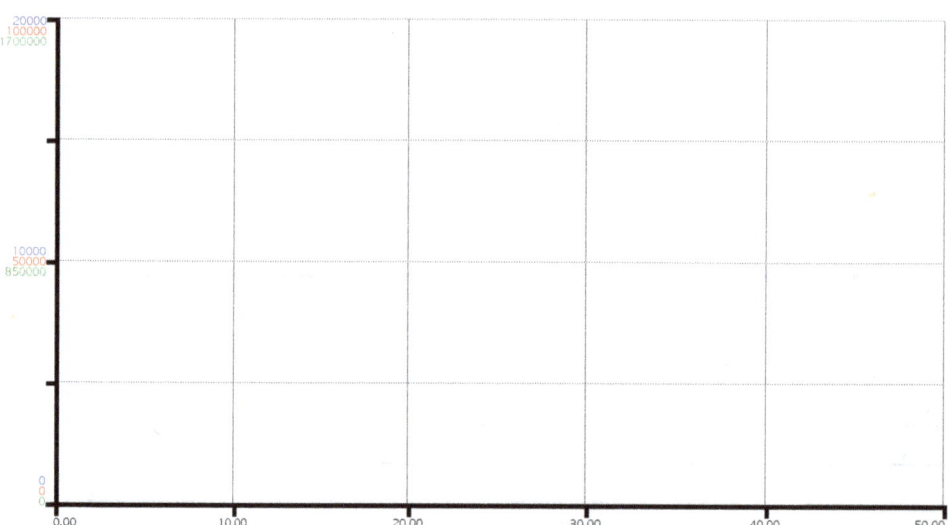

a. Explain what happened and why.

_____
_____
_____
_____

b. **Click** the triangle (bottom left on graph pad) to flip to page 2. Copy that graph below. Then flip to page 3 and copy that graph.

Prey killed vs. Desired prey killed

Livestock and pets killed per year

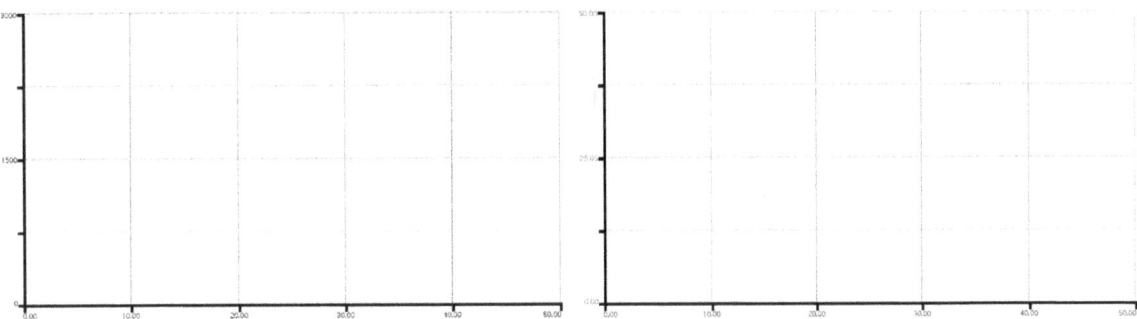

c. How do you think the hunters are feeling? Why?

_____
_____
_____
_____
_____
_____
_____

d. How do you think the farmers and residents are feeling? Why?

_____
_____
_____
_____
_____
_____
_____

e. What changes would you make to improve your results?

_____
_____
_____
_____
_____
_____
_____

Continue running the "Real World," trying different hunting plans. Record your best run on the graphs. Remember your goal is that the populations and food are healthy without too many ups and downs, the hunters can hunt, and the people's animals are safe.

Predators, Prey, and Food

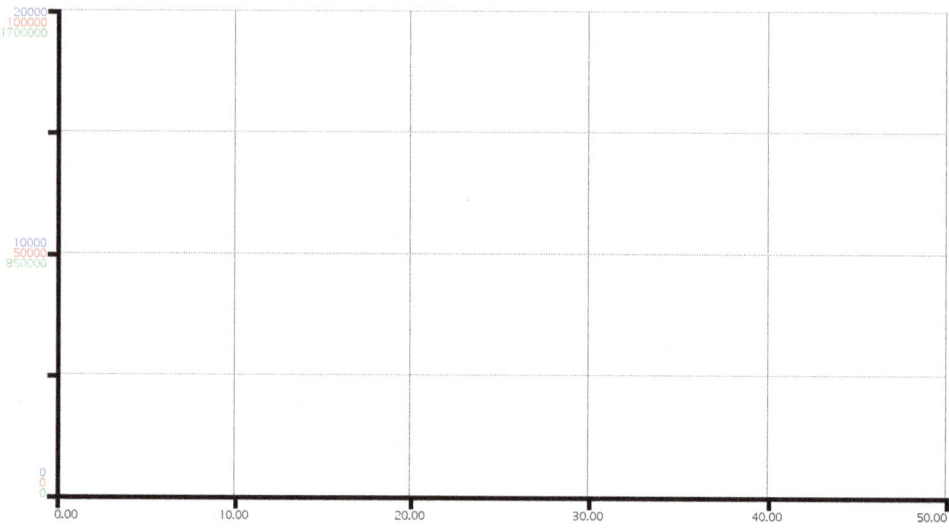

Prey killed vs. Desired prey killed   Livestock and pets killed per year

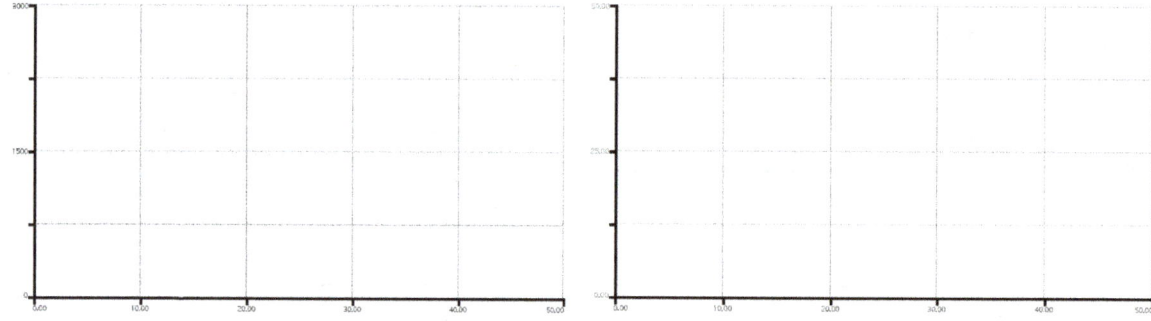

What did you do to get these results?

_____
_____
_____
_____
_____
_____

Predator, Prey and Plants – Debrief

Part I

Go back to the Menu and **click "Debrief."** Explore each of the four sections, answering the questions below.

Click "1. Ecosystem Ups and Downs."

a. What is the term used to describe a graph that goes up and down over time?
_____

b. Draw a graph showing that behavior.

c. How does the "Food for Prey" affect both the predator and prey populations? Look at the graph on the screen to help you.
_____
_____
_____

Click on each of the "Graphs to Explore" and read about each situation. Make sure to read the stories and look at the graphs for hunters/residents/farmers.

d. Which situation do you think is best for keeping the ecosystem healthy? Why?
_____
_____
_____

e. Which situation do you think is best for keeping the people happy? Why?
_____
_____
_____

Click "2. Ecosystems as a Circle." Read the story of the loops. Why do the loops balance over time?
_____
_____
_____

Part II

Click "3. Predator/Prey/Food Map."
How did the four parts you changed on the **Decisions** screen affect the predators, the prey, and the food?

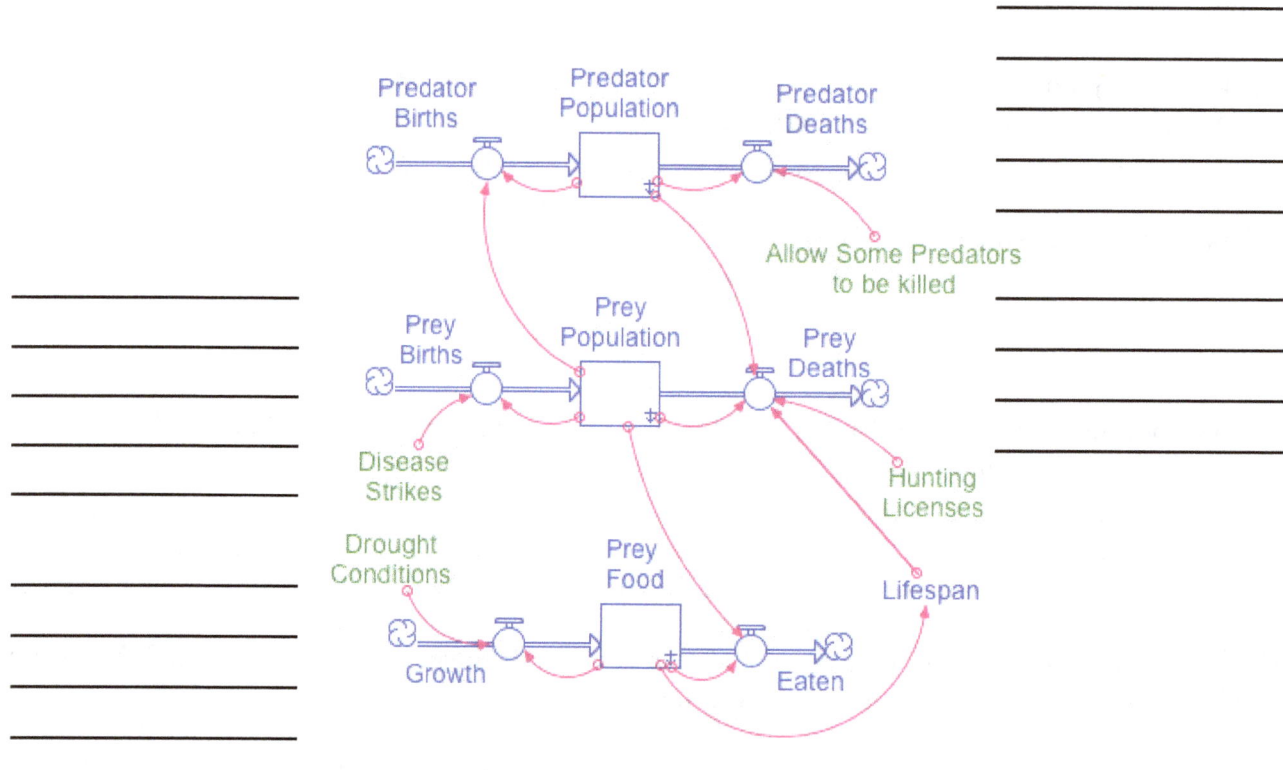

Click "4. Connections." What are some other connections you can see between predator/prey/food relationships and other systems in the world?

LESSON 5, LEVEL B, HANDOUT 4 – P.1

Official Memo

DATE:

TO: **Rutheforest T. Grove, Park Director**

FROM:

REGARDING: **Recommended Plan**

My results: Graphs from the Best "Real World" Run

Predators, Prey, and Food

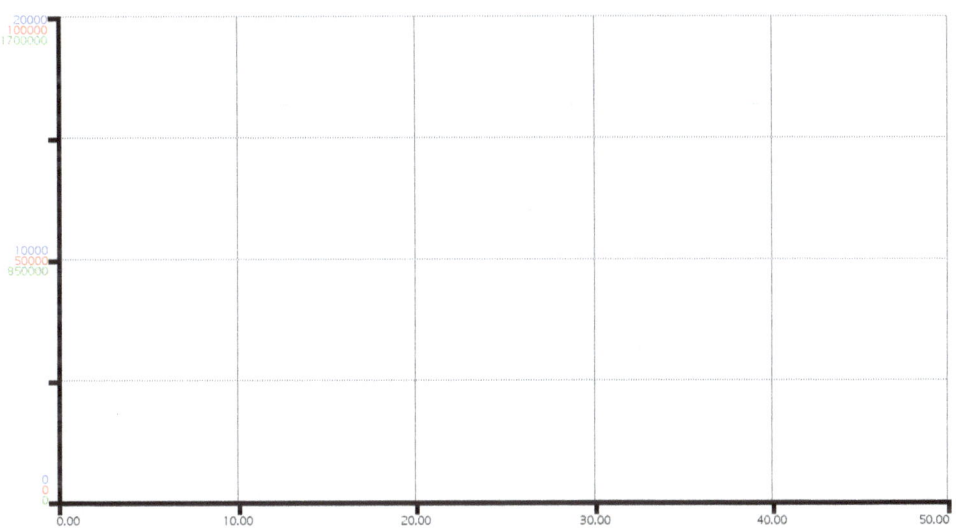

Prey killed vs. Desired prey killed

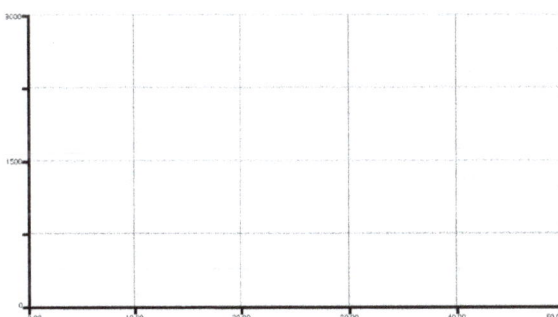

Livestock and pets killed per year

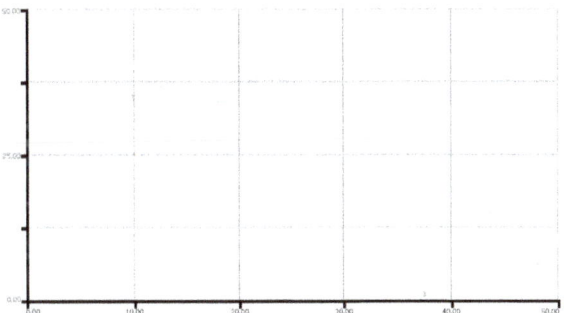

What I did: _____
_____
_____
_____
_____
_____
_____
_____

How I handled complaints:

Year	Complaint and Issues	Action Taken

Recommended Plan:

Policy Areas	What I think the best plan is	Why I think this plan is best for the ecosystem and the people
#1 – Hunting prey (moose)		
#2 – Killing predators (wolves)		
#3 – Complaints from hunters		
#4 – Complaints from farmers/ residents		

LESSON 5, LEVEL B, HANDOUT 5

Predator, Prey and Plants – Optional Assessment

Describe the story of the loops. Make sure to write about each part and how it affects any other parts.

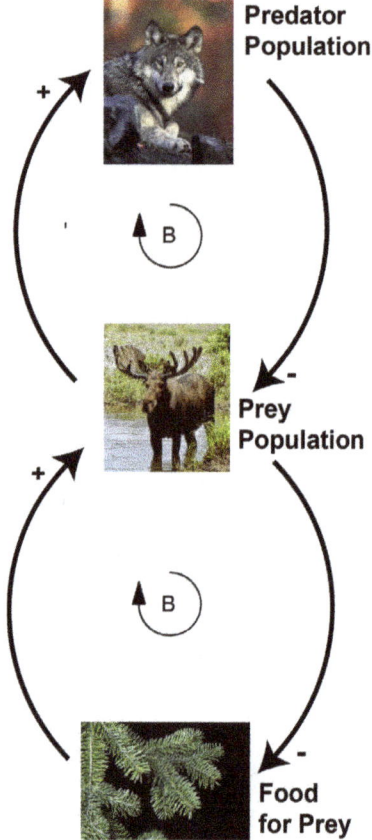

Lesson 6 – Level B
Running in Circles: How Fast Can We Go?

Overview

This lesson explores individual choices and work styles, and how some of those choices may lead to cycles of burnout. Students take on the role of "advisor" to friends who are experiencing these cycles and also reflect on their own personal life choices.

Learning Goals

- Represent and interpret data on a line graph.
- Explore possible causes of burnout and identify potential leverage for prevention.
- Give advice to "friends" based on an understanding of causes and leverage points.
- Self-assess, reflect, and make a personal plan.

FIGURE 1: Title Screen

Student Challenge

Explore a series of situations, giving advice to virtual "friends" who are experiencing burnout cycles.

LESSON 6 – LEVEL B – AGES 8+

Time
3 or more 45-minute sessions

Materials
- One computer for every 2–3 students
- Handouts (See pages 78–95)

Curricular Connections
- Math: Representing and interpreting data*
- Reading: Describing connections between ideas*
- Science: Feedback mechanisms, motivation of organisms
- Social Studies: Individual development and identity

*Common Core State Standards

Key system dynamics concepts and insights
- Energy and participation levels affect one another and can create cycles of burnout over time.
- Both energy recovery and energy drain are affected by activity.
- Leverage for preventing burnout includes limiting hours of activity.

Additional information, based on Level C simulation

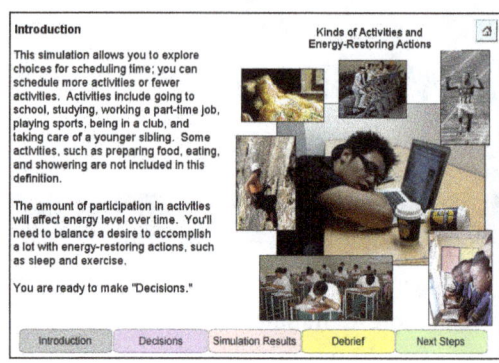

FIGURE 2: Introduction

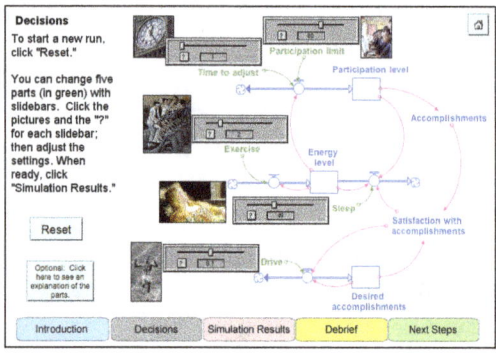

FIGURE 3: Decisions

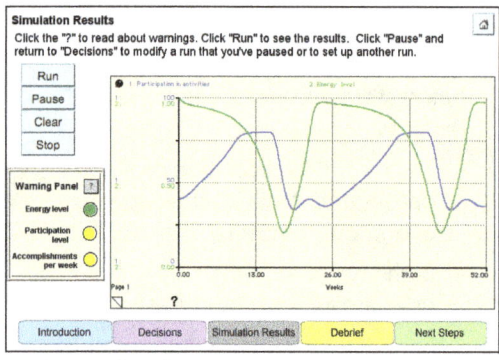

FIGURE 4: Simulation Results

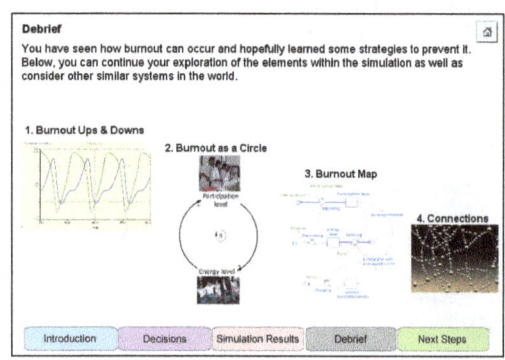

FIGURE 5: Debrief

Lesson Details

Preparation

1. Create groups of 2–3 students each.
2. Copy all handouts for each student or student group.
3. Check computers to make sure you can access the online simulation.

Session 1

1. Introduce vocabulary as needed, including cycle, burnout, and types of participation in activities (e.g., going to school, studying, working a part-time job, being in a club, and taking care of a younger sibling).
2. Describe the project in which students will put together final recommendations for the case studies and also for themselves. Go over the requirements and rubric (Handout 1, page 78).
3. Have students open the simulation and read the introduction (Handout 1 and Figure 2).
4. Students can now set up the simulation on the "Decisions" screens (Figure 3). As they do this, have students record data and reflections as they work through the experimental stage and case studies in the handouts (Handout 2, pages 80–90 and Figure 4).

Session 2

1. If needed, have students complete the simulation within their small groups.
2. After working through the case studies and personal reflection, students can continue to the "Debrief" section (Handout 3, pages 91–92 and Figure 5).
3. Debrief the simulation experience using ideas for bringing the lesson home and assessment ideas. The key assessment in this lesson is a write-up of final recommendations that summarize the student's learning (Handout 4, pages 93–94).
4. A second, optional assessment allows students to show their understanding of the interconnections among the main simulation elements (Handout 5, page 95). See below for one possible "story" of the loop.

Example Story: Participation level represents how much a person is doing. Energy level represents how good people feel, physically. Are they feeling really energetic or are they tired? These affect one another.

If participation goes up, energy drains out. If energy goes down, participation goes down, too. People are too tired to do much, so they stop.

Once they decrease how much they are doing, they can recover some energy. If energy is higher, people can again do more, so participation goes up.

Bringing the Lesson Home

- Have students explore the "Debrief" and "Next Steps" sections of the simulation within their small group or as a class (Handout 3, pages 91–92). Note that some of the resources on the "Next Steps" section are YouTube videos.
- Discuss the trends on the graphs and the interconnections among the parts.
    - What caused the burnout oscillations?
    - How do the various elements increase or decrease the likelihood of burnout occurring?
    - What are the key leverage points for preventing burnout?
    - How do these ideas connect to what people expect of one another?

Assessment Ideas

- Create a write-up of final recommendations for "friends" and also for self. (Handout 4, pages 93–94).
- Describe the interactions among the main simulation elements (Handout 5, page 95).

ACKNOWLEDGEMENTS

Lesson 6 – Level B • Running in Circles: How Fast Can We Go? ©2014 Creative Learning Exchange
This model is one in a series of models that explores the characteristics of complex systems.

Model created with contributions from Jen Andersen, Anne LaVigne, Michael Radzicki, George Richardson, Lees Stuntz, and with support from Jay Forrester and the Creative Learning Exchange.

Image Credits
Wolf, Gary Kramer, USFWS, Public Domain.
Balsam Fir, USDA, Public Domain.
Moose, USFWS, Public Domain.
Spider web, USFWS, Public Domain.
Lit Match, Sebastian Ritter, Wikimedia Commons Attribution-Share Alike 2.5 Generic. (http://creativecommons.org/licenses/by-sa/2.5/deed.en)
Boy sleeping, by Shanghai killer whale, Wikimedia Commons, Creative Commons Attribution-Share Alike 3.0 Unported. (http://creativecommons.org/licenses/by-sa/3.0/deed.en)
Sleeping Beauty painting, John Collier, Public Domain.
Exercise machines, Henry M. Trotter, Wikimedia Commons, Public Domain.
Billy Mills, U.S. Marine Corp., Public Domain.
Rock climber, Geof Sheppard, Wikimedia Commons, Creative Commons Attribution-ShareAlike 3.0 Unported license.
Classroom, Dennis Kwaria, Wikimedia Commons, Creative Commons Attribution-Share Alike 3.0.
Kids on computers, IICD.org, Wikimedia Commons, Creative Commons Attribution 2.0 Generic.
Clock, by Arpingstone, Wikimedia Commons, Public Domain.
Students in lab, Dennis Kwaria, Wikimedia Commons, Creative Commons 1.0 Universal Public Domain Dedication. (http://creativecommons.org/publicdomain/zero/1.0/deed.en)
Students on bench, Dennis Kwaria, Wikimedia Commons, Creative Commons Attribution-Share Alike 3.0 Unported.
The Scream, Edvard Munch, Public Domain.
Two kids on game system, by Arpingstone, Wikimedia Commons, Public Domain.
Rocks, by Seventhrunner, Wikimedia Commons, Public Domain.

LESSON 6, LEVEL B, HANDOUT 1 – P.1

Running in Circles – Introduction

Some of your friends have asked you for advice. You will use this simulation to help them think about choices they make in their lives and how those choices may affect what they are able to do and their energy levels. At the end, you'll write your final recommendations.

Parts of the project:
1. Title page
   - Title: Running in Circles: How Fast Can We Go?
   - Name and date
   - An illustration of life choices related to school, work, and play
     You can create a collage, drawing, or other representation to show the parts of the system and how they are connected.
2. Handouts 1–3, complete and organized neatly in order
   - Handout 1 – Introduction, Rubric, and Instructions
   - Handout 2 – Experimental Runs and Case Studies
   - Handout 3 – Debrief
3. Handout 4 – Final recommendations for each student and your personal plan
4. Handout 5 – Assessment

Project Assessment Rubric

	Novice	**Basic**	**Proficient**	**Advanced**
Title Page	My pictures are not about the system.	I have pictures, but I didn't show any connections.	My pictures show important parts of the system and how they are connected.	In addition, I added words to explain the connections.
Handouts	I didn't explain what happened.	I recorded results that were mostly accurate. I explained what happened.	I recorded results that were accurate. I clearly explained what happened and why.	In addition, I met each challenge and explained why I was successful.
Recommendations (RECs)	My RECs are missing or very little is included to show my learning.	I wrote RECs, but I did not include proof from the simulation.	I wrote clear RECs and included proof from the simulation.	In addition, I gave real-life examples of the RECs.

LESSON 6, LEVEL B, HANDOUT 1 – P.2

Click the picture of the burning match.
What is the definition of burnout in your own words? _____
_____

Click the **Start** button. **Read** the "**Introduction**" screen and click on the pictures.

What is the definition of an activity in this simulation? _____
_____

What is an example of an activity? _____

What is an activity that's not included in this definition? _____

Click "Decisions." **Click** the question marks (**?**) and pictures for each of the decisions. After reading each one, write a definition in your own words and give an example.

Participation limit _____
_____

   Example: _____

Time to adjust _____
_____

   Example: _____

Exercise _____
_____

   Example: _____

Sleep _____
_____

   Example: _____

Drive _____
_____

   Example: _____

Running in Circles – Exploration

Experimental Runs

Do several runs with different settings. Just experiment and see what you can discover about what happens with different settings. When you feel you know enough to give your friends some advice, write a summary of your learning below and proceed to your first "case." Make sure to include what causes the ups and downs of burnout in the simulation.

What I've learned so far:

_____
_____
_____
_____
_____
_____
_____
_____
_____
_____
_____
_____
_____
_____
_____
_____
_____
_____
_____

Case Studies:
Friend #1 – Raven
Friend #2 – Sammy
Friend #3 – Evelyn
Friend #4 – Oxford
My Pattern

LESSON 6, LEVEL B, HANDOUT 2 – P.2

Friend #1 – Raven

Raven is an extremely ambitious student. She will be the first person in her family to attend college, and both she and everyone around her have very high expectations. Because of her drive to do more and more no matter what, she has been having some problems with keeping promises over the last year. Her family is very worried, because she's always stayed on top of responsibilities in the past.

Set the simulation as shown below and then **Run**.

Slider	Setting
Participation limit	90 hours/week
Time to adjust	1 week
Exercise	2 hours/week
Sleep	35 hours/week
Drive	0.2 (very high)

Record your results on the graphs below. Make sure to create labels and a key for each graph. Note that you'll need to **click** the bottom-left corner of the graph to see Page 2.

Participation in activities and Energy level

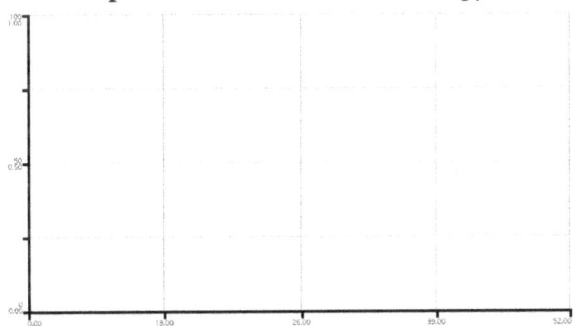

Accomplishments per week and to date

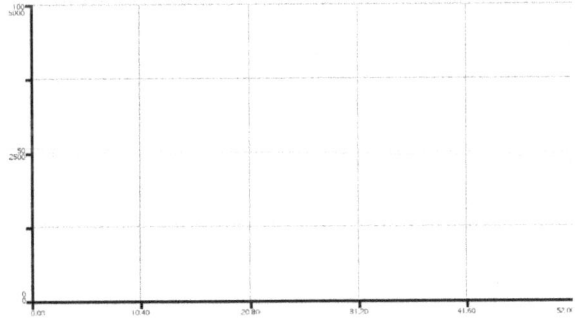

LESSON 6, LEVEL B, HANDOUT 2 – P.3

a. Why do you think Raven experiencing cycles of burnout?
_____
_____
_____

b. Raven wants to stop the cycles, but she still wants to achieve a lot. What are some ideas that would help her stop the crazy ups and downs, while still keeping accomplishments high?
_____
_____
_____

Continue running the simulation, trying different plans for Raven. Record the graphs for your best run below.

Participation in activities and Energy level

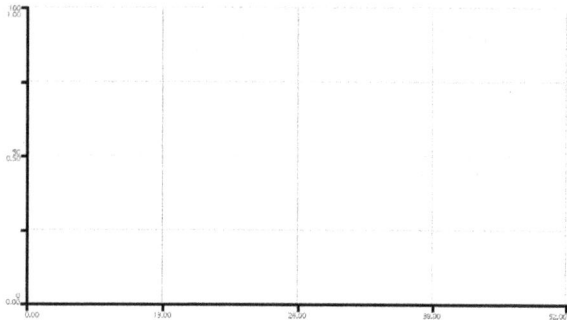

c. What were the new settings?

Slider	Setting
Participation limit	
Time to adjust	
Exercise	
Sleep	
Drive	

Accomplishments per week and to date

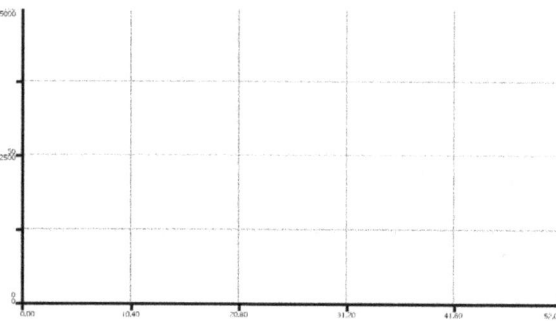

d. What changes would you really need to make in your life in order to accomplish this?
_____
_____
_____
_____
_____
_____

Friend #2 – Sammy

Sammy has a high drive, but he also finds time to exercise and get plenty of sleep. His goal is to make the next Olympics team in gymnastics. Unfortunately, he still has periods of exhaustion. This causes him to lose interest in working so hard; he stops showing up for practice and is also having trouble keeping up in school.

Set the simulation as shown below and then **Run**.

Slider	Setting
Participation limit	100 hours/week
Time to adjust	1 week
Exercise	10 hours/week
Sleep	60 hours/week
Drive	0.2 (very high)

Record your results on the graphs below. Make sure to create labels and a key for each graph. Note that you'll need to **click** the bottom-left corner of the graph to see Page 2.

Participation in activities and Energy level

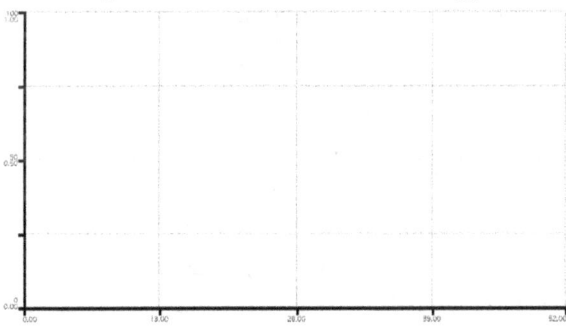

Accomplishments per week and to date

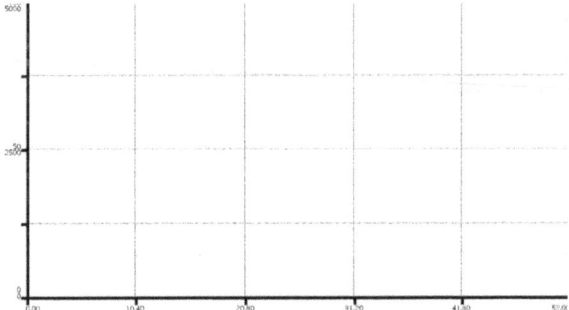

a. Why do you think Sammy is experiencing cycles of burnout?
_____
_____
_____

b. Sammy wants to stop the cycles, but he still wants to make the team. What are some ideas that would help him stop the crazy ups and downs, while still keeping his chances high for making the Olympic team?
_____
_____
_____

Continue running the simulation, trying different plans for Sammy. Record the graphs for your best run below.

Participation in activities and Energy level

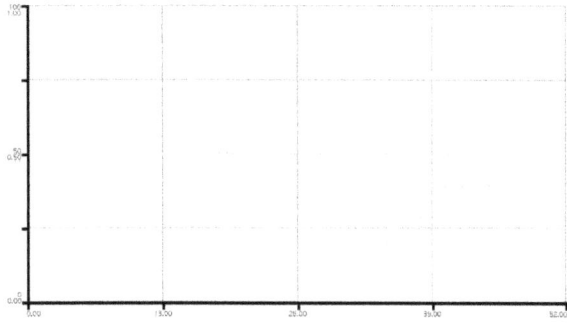

c. What were the new settings?

Slider	Setting
Participation limit	
Time to adjust	
Exercise	
Sleep	
Drive	

Accomplishments per week and to date

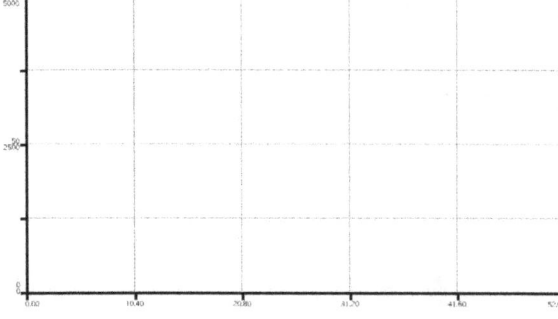

d. What changes would Sammy really need to make in his life in order to accomplish this?
_____
_____
_____
_____
_____
_____
_____

Friend #3 – Evelyn

Evelyn has some drive, and she has a hard time saying no to other people's requests. Because of this, her participation limit is high. She also doesn't find the time to exercise because she is always doing tasks for other people.

Set the simulation as shown below and then **Run**.

Slider	Setting
Participation limit	80 hours/week
Time to adjust	1 week
Exercise	0 hours/week
Sleep	40 hours/week
Drive	0.1 (some)

Record your results on the graphs below. Make sure to create labels and a key for each graph. Note that you'll need to **click** the bottom-left corner of the graph to see Page 2.

Participation in activities and Energy level

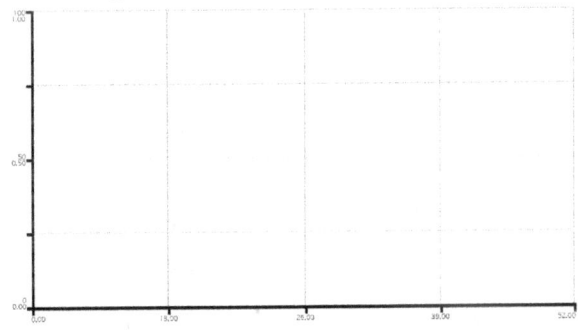

Accomplishments per week and to date

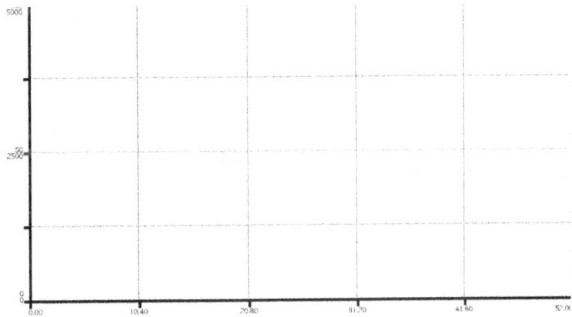

LESSON 6, LEVEL B, HANDOUT 2 – P.7

a. Why do you think Evelyn is experiencing cycles of burnout?
_____
_____
_____

b. Evelyn wants to stop the cycles, but she still wants to achieve a lot. What are some ideas that would help her stop the crazy ups and downs, while still letting her help others from time to time?
_____
_____
_____

Continue running the simulation, trying different plans for Evelyn. Record the graphs for your best run below.

Participation in activities and Energy level

c. What were the new settings?

Slider	Setting
Participation limit	
Time to adjust	
Exercise	
Sleep	
Drive	

Accomplishments per week and to date

d. What changes would Evelyn really need to make in her life in order to accomplish this?
_____
_____
_____
_____
_____
_____

LESSON 6, LEVEL B, HANDOUT 2 – P.8

Friend #4 – Oxford
Oxford has no drive at the moment. He wants to do more than he's currently doing but could use some advice. He does not want to turn his life into "Work, Work, Work!" He's seen what has happened to some of his friends; it seems to him they have no life.

Set the simulation as shown below and then **Run**.

Slider	Setting
Participation limit	40 hours/week
Time to adjust	1 week
Exercise	5 hours/week
Sleep	70 hours/week
Drive	0 (none)

Record your results on the graphs below. Make sure to create labels and a key for each graph. Note that you'll need to **click** the bottom-left corner of the graph to see Page 2.

Participation in activities and Energy level

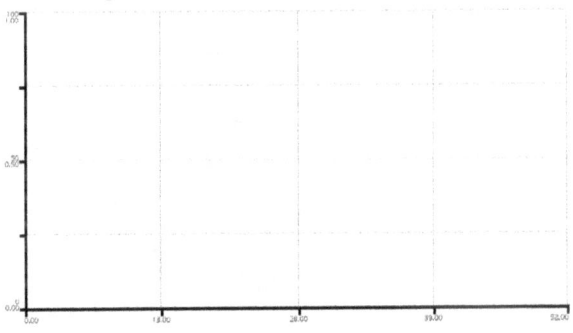

Accomplishments per week and to date

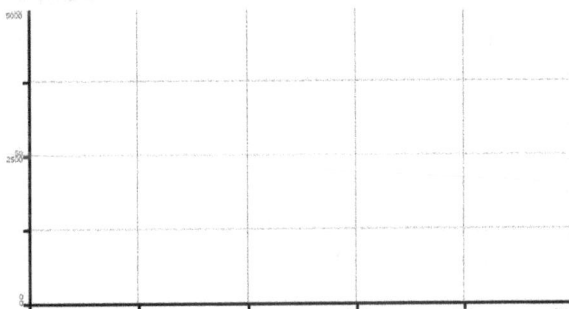

LESSON 6, LEVEL B, HANDOUT 2 – P.9

a. Why do you think Oxford is not experiencing cycles of burnout?
_____
_____
_____

b. Oxford want to increase his accomplishments, but not by exhausting himself. What are some ideas that would help him increase success, while still preventing burnout cycles?
_____
_____
_____
_____

Continue running the simulation, trying different plans for Oxford. Record the graphs for your best run below.

Participation in activities and Energy level

c. What were the new settings?

Slider	Setting
Participation limit	
Time to adjust	
Exercise	
Sleep	
Drive	

Accomplishments per week and to date

d. What changes would Oxford really need to make in his life in order to accomplish this?
_____
_____
_____
_____
_____
_____

88 • LESSON 6 – Level B • Running in Circles   ©2014 Creative Learning Exchange

My Pattern

What's your story? _____

_____

_____

_____

_____

_____

Set the simulation based on your story and record the settings.

Slider	Setting
Participation limit	hours/week
Time to adjust	week
Exercise	hours/week
Sleep	hours/week
Drive	

Record your results on the graphs below. Make sure to create labels and a key for each graph. Note that you'll need to **click** the bottom-left corner of the graph to see Page 2.

Participation in activities and Energy level

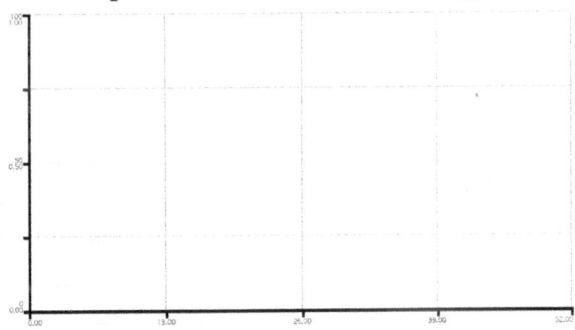

Accomplishments per week and to date

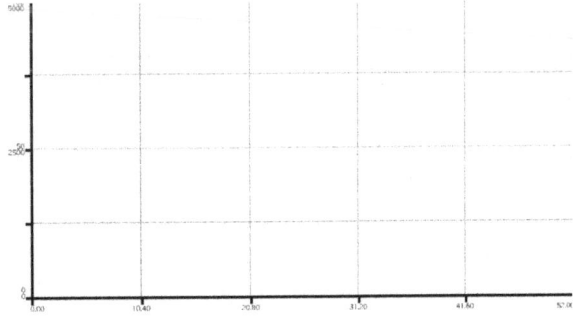

LESSON 6, LEVEL B, HANDOUT 2 – P.11

a. What's happing on your graphs? Are cycles of burnout happening?
_____
_____
_____

b. How accurate are the graphs in comparison to what's really happening in your life?
_____
_____
_____

c. What, if any, changes would you like to see? If none, please explain why. Try some different ideas using the simulation, and then record your favorite run below.
_____
_____
_____

Participation in activities and Energy level

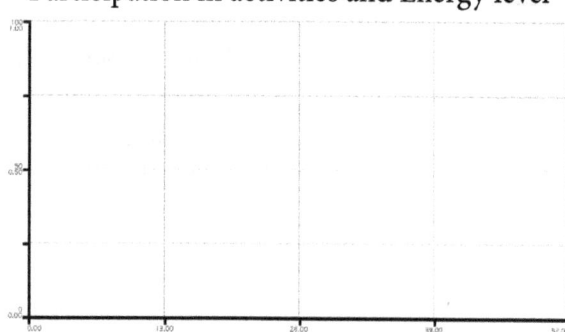

d. What were the new settings?

Slider	Setting
Participation limit	
Time to adjust	
Exercise	
Sleep	
Drive	

Accomplishments per week and to date

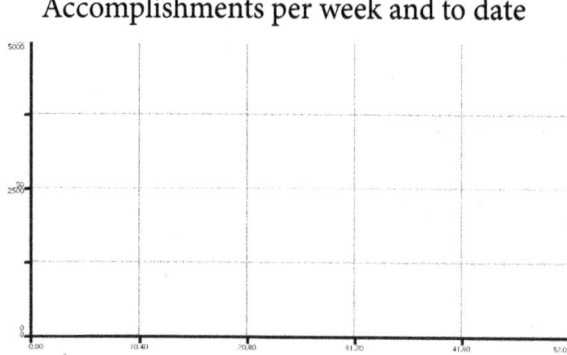

e. What changes would you really need to make in your life in order to accomplish this?
_____
_____
_____
_____
_____
_____

Running in Circles – Debrief

Part I

Go back to the Menu and **click "Debrief."** Explore each of the four sections, answering the questions below.

Click "1. Burnout Ups & Downs."
Look at each of the example situations. Make sure to read each of the stories and look at the graphs for accomplishments.

a. Which situation allowed the person to accomplish the most? Why?
_____
_____
_____
_____

b. Which situation do you think is best for keeping people happy and healthy? Why?
_____
_____
_____
_____

c. Which situation is closest to your own pattern? In what ways?
_____
_____
_____
_____

Click "2. Burnout as a Circle."
Read the story of the loop.
a. Why does the loop create ups and downs over time?
_____
_____
_____

b. What's one example of this loop in your own life experience?
_____
_____
_____

LESSON 6, LEVEL B, HANDOUT 3 – P.2

Part II

Click "3. Burnout Map."
Read and **click "Next Part."** **Click** the map and unfold the story.

How did the five parts you changed affect desired accomplishments, participation level, and energy level?

Time to adjust:
_____
_____
_____
_____

Exercise:
_____
_____
_____
_____

Drive:
_____
_____
_____
_____

Participation limit:
_____
_____
_____
_____

Sleep:
_____
_____
_____
_____

Click "4. Connections."
What are some other connections you can see between burnout cycles and other systems in the world?
_____
_____
_____
_____
_____
_____
_____
_____

92 • LESSON 6 – Level B • Running in Circles

Running in Circles – Final Recommendations

Student	What I think is the best plan	Why this plan is best for this person (Include proof and examples.)
Student #1 – Raven		
Student #2 – Sammy		
Student #3 – Evelyn		

Student	What I think is the best plan	Why this plan is best for this person (Include proof and examples.)
Student #4 – Oxford		
Me		

LESSON 6, LEVEL B, HANDOUT 5

Running in Circles – Assessment

Describe the story of the loop. Make sure to write about each part and how it affects the other part.

Participation level

+

B

−

Energy level

_____

_____

What could you add to this loop to make the story even better? Draw ideas on the back and explain below.

_____

©2014 Creative Learning Exchange   LESSON 6 – Level B • Running in Circles • 95

Lesson 7 – Level B

From Farm to Table: The Ups and Downs of What We Buy

Overview

This lesson explores a commodity market, hog farming, from two different perspectives. Students experience a simulated large and small farm, comparing the similarities and differences among trends, including retail pork prices and availability of pork.

Learning Goals

- Represent and interpret data on a line graph.
- Describe possible causes of oscillating price, demand, and supply by comparing simulated large and small hog farms.
- Write an editorial article based on simulation trends.

FIGURE 1: Title Screen

Student Challenge

Investigate different types of hog farms and write an editorial article with findings.

LESSON 7 – LEVEL B – AGES 8+

Time
Three or more 45-minute sessions

Materials
- One computer for every 2–3 students
- Handouts (See pages 101–112)

Curricular Connections
- Math: Representing and interpreting data*
- Reading: Describing connections among ideas*
- National Curriculum Standards for Social Studies: Characteristics of a market economy, how people deal with scarcity of resources, how consumers react to rising/falling prices of goods.

*Common Core State Standards

Key system dynamics concepts and insights
- Interdependencies exist among inventory, demand, and price and tend to create oscillations over time.
- Supply of a product cannot be increased or decreased instantaneously; delays exist.

Additional information, based on Level C simulation

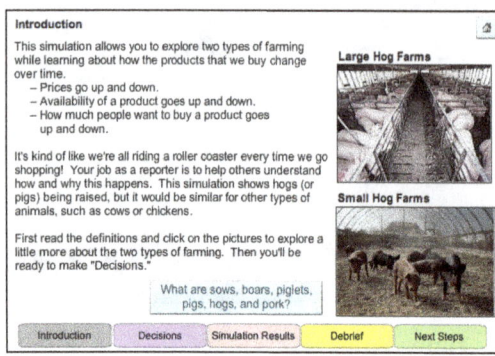

FIGURE 2: Introduction

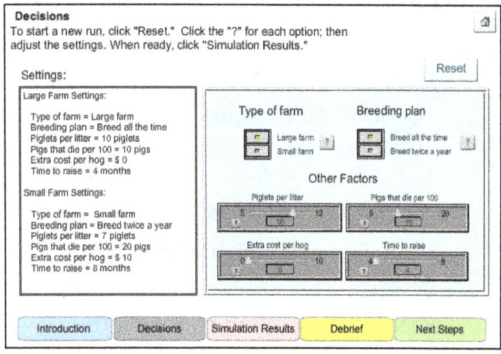

FIGURE 3: Decisions

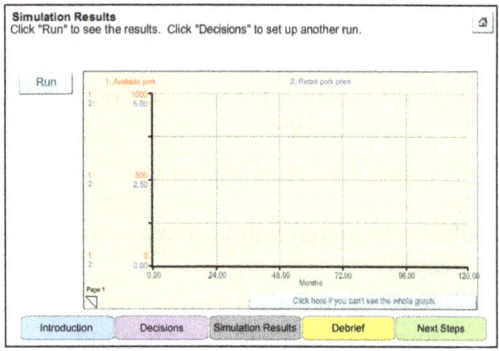

FIGURE 4: Simulation Results

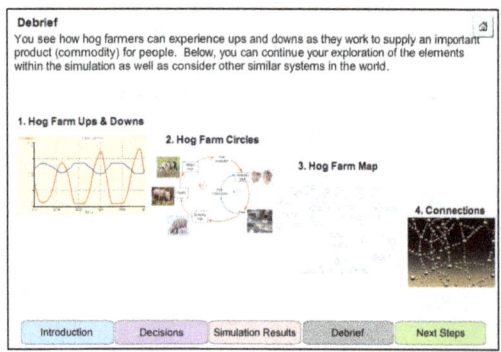

FIGURE 5: Debrief

Lesson Details

Preparation

1. Create groups of 2–3 students each.
2. Copy all handouts for each student or student group.
3. Check computers to make sure you can access the online simulation.

Session 1:

1. Introduce vocabulary as needed including product, commodity, scarcity, supply, demand, price, inventory, consumers, and market economy.
2. Describe the project in which students will take on the role of reporter and write an editorial article for a local newspaper. As part of the article, they will describe the two methods of farming and make a recommendation to the "readers." Go over the requirements and rubric. (Handout 1, page 101)
3. Have students open the simulation and read the introduction. (Handout 1 and Figure 2).
4. Students can now set up the simulation on the "Decisions" screens (Figure 3). As they do this, have students record data and reflections as they work through the scenarios in the handouts (Handout 2, pages 103–108 and Figure 4).

Session 2:

1. If needed, have students complete the simulation within their small groups.
2. After working through the scenarios, students can continue to the "Debrief" section (Handout 3 and Figure 5).
3. Debrief the simulation experience using ideas for bringing the lesson home and assessment ideas. The key assessment within this lesson is the editorial article, backed up with evidence from the simulation. Handout 4 (page 111) is intended as a pre-writing tool. Students may need additional information about what to include in this type of article. Note that the simulation is not intended to convince students that one method is better than another. Both methods have benefits and tradeoffs for people, animals, and the environment. The different scenarios are intended to promote discussion around this complex issue with multiple perspectives.

4. A second, optional assessment allows students to show their understanding of the interconnections among the main simulation elements (Handout 5). See below for one possible "story" of the loop.

Example Story: As the price rises, farmers increase breeding hogs. This allows for more piglets to be born. These piglets grow into full size mature hogs.

After hogs reach a large enough size, they are killed and processed into pork. The more pork that's available for customers, the more the price will fall.

At the same time, if the price goes up too much, people choose to eat less pork. It's just too expensive! This means there will be more pork available, which will cause the price to go down. The store will have to have a sale, because there's too much.

Bringing the Lesson Home

- Have students explore the "Debrief" and "Next Steps" sections (Handout 3). Note that some resources on the "Next Steps" section are YouTube videos.
- Discuss graph trends and interconnections among the parts.
  - What causes price and available pork oscillations?
  - What causes different trends for small vs. large farms?
  - What are key leverage points for preventing wild price oscillations?
  - How does the hog market compare to other markets? Other systems?
  - What are benefits and tradeoffs of each farming method?
  - How practical is a small farming method in terms of feeding the population as a whole?

Assessment Ideas

- Write an editorial article.
- Describe the interactions among the main simulation elements. (Handout 5, page 112).

ACKNOWLEDGEMENTS

Lesson 7 – Level B • From Farm to Table: The Ups and Downs of What We Buy
©2014 Creative Learning Exchange
This model is one in a series of models that explores the characteristics of complex systems.

Model created with contributions from Jen Andersen, Anne LaVigne, Michael Radzicki, George Richardson, Lees Stuntz, and with support from Jay Forrester and the Creative Learning Exchange.

Image Credits

Hogs in barn - EPA, Wikimedia Commons, Public Domain.
Pigs in hoop house – by Brian Johnson & Dane Kantner, Creative Commons Attribution 2.0 Generic license (http://creativecommons.org/licenses/by/2.0/deed.en).
Chickens, by Jessica Reeder, Wikimedia Commons, Creative Commons Attribution 2.0 Generic license (http://creativecommons.org/licenses/by/2.0/deed.en).
Amish farm, by vishwin60, Wikimedia Commons, Public Domain.
Landrace boar, by Dingar, Wikimedia Commons, Public Domain.
Piglets standing, USDA, Public Domain.
Pork, by Amidelalune, Wikimedia Commons, Public Domain.
Four sows in pen, by Guido Gerding, Wikimedia Commons, Creative Commons Attribution -ShareAlike 3.0 Unported license (http://creativecommons.org/licenses/by-sa/3.0/deed.en)
Large black pigs and Gloucester Boar, by Amanda Slater, Wikimedia Commons, Creative Commons Attribution 2.0 Generic license (http://creativecommons.org/licenses/by/2.0/deed.en)
Meat counter, Southern Foodways Alliance, Wikimedia Commons, Creative Commons Attribution 2.0 Generic license (http://creativecommons.org/licenses/by/2.0/deed.en)
Sow with one nursing piglet, by Scott Bauer, USDA, Wikimedia Commons, Public Domain.
Black/pink sow with piglets, by Joy Schoenberger, Wikimedia Commons, GNU Free Documentation, http://commons.wikimedia.org/wiki/GNU_Free_Documentation_License
Pink pigs in field, by Jessica Reeder, Wikimedia Commons, Creative Commons Attribution 2.0 Generic license (http://creativecommons.org/licenses/by/2.0/deed.en).
Hand holding spring, by Anne LaVigne, Used with permission.
Spider web, USFWS, Public Domain.
City, Detroit Publishing Company, Wikimedia Commons, Public Domain.
Boy with toy, WP Van de Hoef, Wikimedia Commons, Public Domain.

Other Credits

National Curriculum Standards for Social Studies, National Council for Social Studies. 2010.

From Farm to Table – Introduction

You have just been hired by a newspaper to write an editorial article about hog farming. An editorial is an opinion article backed up with proof of your opinion. In this case, you will use this simulation to learn about large and small hog farms. At the end, you'll write your article comparing the two types of farming and giving your opinion about what type works best.

Parts of the project

1. Handouts 1-5, complete and organized neatly in order
   - Handout 1 – Introduction, Rubric, and Instructions
   - Handout 2 – Scenario Runs
   - Handout 3 – Debrief
   - Handout 4 – Farm Comparison
   - Handout 5 – Assessment
2. Editorial Article
   - Article title
   - Name and "date of publication"
   - 500–1000 word article (Make sure to use Handout 4 to help you write your article.)
3. Illustration for your article
   - An illustration that shows the basic issue described within the article. You can create a collage, drawing, or other representation.

Project Assessment Rubric

	Novice	Basic	Proficient	Advanced
Handouts	I didn't explain what happened.	I recorded results that were mostly accurate. I explained what happened.	I recorded results that were accurate. I clearly explained what happened and why.	In addition, I am able to meet each challenge and can explain why I was successful.
Editorial Article	My article is missing or very little is included to show my learning.	I wrote an article with some facts I learned, but I did not include proof from the simulation.	I wrote a clear article with a well-defined opinion and included proof from the simulation.	In addition, I gave proof by connecting learning from the simulation to other similar systems.
Title Page	My pictures are not about the system.	I have pictures, but I didn't show any connections.	My pictures have important parts of the system and how they are connected.	In addition, I have added words to explain the connections.

LESSON 7, LEVEL B, HANDOUT 1 – P.2

Click the **Start** button. Read the **Introduction** screen, the definitions, and the description of large and small farms.

a. What are ways that products people buy change over time? _____
_____

b. What is one product that you buy that has changed in one of these ways. Describe the details.
_____
_____
_____

Fill in the following:
Sows and Boars → _____ → _____ ↓
↑
_____ ← _____ ← _____

c. What are characteristics of a large farm in this simulation? _____
_____
_____

d. What are characteristics of a small farm in this simulation? _____
_____
_____

e. **Click Decisions. Click** the question marks (**?**) for each decision and write a definition in your own words.

Breeding plan _____
_____

Piglets per litter _____
_____

Piglets that die per 100 _____
_____

Extra cost per hog _____
_____

Time to raise _____
_____

LESSON 7, LEVEL B, HANDOUT 2 – P.1

From Farm to Table – Scenarios

Scenario #1 – Large Farms

a. Given the settings below, what do you predict will happen to the availability of pork and the retail pork price over time?

_____
_____
_____
_____
_____

b. Set the simulation as shown below and then run.

Decision	Setting
Type of farm	large
Breeding plan	breed all the time
Piglets per litter	10 piglets
Pigs that die per 100	10 pigs
Extra cost per hog	$ 0
Time to raise	4 months

c. Record your results on the graphs below. Make sure to create labels and a key for each graph.

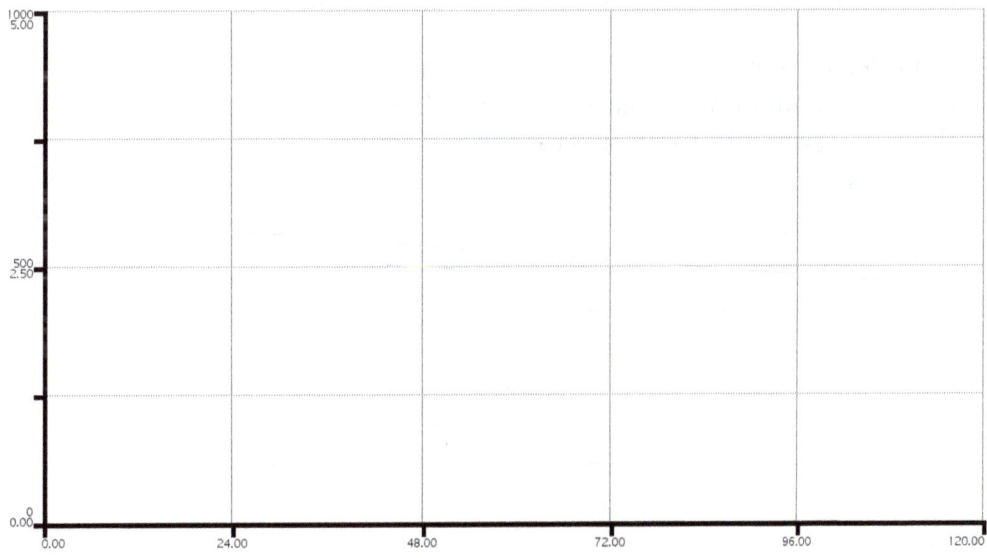

Availability of pork and Retail pork price

©2014 Creative Learning Exchange

LESSON 7, LEVEL B, HANDOUT 2 – P.2

d. What happened to the availability of pork and retail price over time?
_____
_____
_____
_____

e. Why do you think this occurred? Include specific information about how the large farm settings affected the situation.
_____
_____
_____
_____
_____
_____
_____
_____

Click on the bottom-left corner of the graph to see Page two.
f. What happened to the number of piglets, mature hogs, and available pork over time?
_____
_____
_____
_____

g. How do these graphs relate to the retail pork price graph?
_____
_____
_____
_____

Click on the bottom-left corner of the graph to see Page three.
h. Did the farmers make money on the sale of pork over time? Use the graph to explain your response. Notice that the break-even point shows zero profit. Anything above that line is profit. Anything below the line is a loss.
_____
_____
_____
_____
_____
_____
_____

Scenario #2 – Small Farms

a. Given the settings below, what do you predict will happen to the availability of pork and the retail pork price over time?

_____
_____
_____
_____
_____
_____
_____

b. Set the simulation as shown below and then run.

Decision	Setting
Type of farm	small
Breeding plan	breed twice a year
Piglets per litter	7 piglets
Pigs that die per 100	20 pigs
Extra cost per hog	$ 8
Time to raise	8 months

c. Record your results on the graphs below. Make sure to create labels and a key for each graph.

Availability of pork and Retail pork price

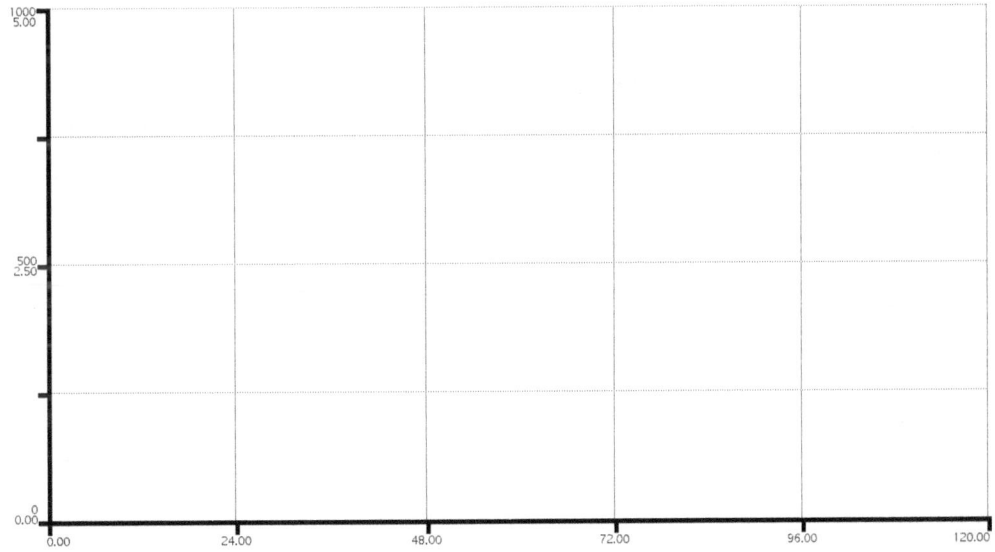

LESSON 7, LEVEL B, HANDOUT 2 – P.4

d. What happened to the availability of pork and retail price over time?

e. Why do you think this occurred? Include specific information about how the small farm settings affected the situation.

Click on the bottom-left corner of the graph to see Page two.
f. What happened to the number of piglets, mature hogs, and available pork over time?

g. How do these graphs relate to the retail pork price graph?

Click on the bottom-left corner of the graph to see Page three.
h. Did the farmers make money on the sale of pork over time? Use the graph to explain your response. Notice that the break-even point shows zero profit. Anything above that line is profit. Anything below the line is a loss.

Scenario #3 – My Own Settings

a. Now it's your turn to set up a farm. You can set up the simulation however you'd like, but consider whether the settings will work in real life.

b. Set up the simulation, record your settings, predict, and then run.
   Prediction for availability of pork and retail pork price:

Decision	Setting
Type of farm	
Breeding plan	
Piglets per litter	
Pigs that die per 100	
Extra cost per hog	
Time to raise	

c. Record your results on the graphs below. Make sure to create labels and a key for each graph.

Availability of pork and Retail pork price

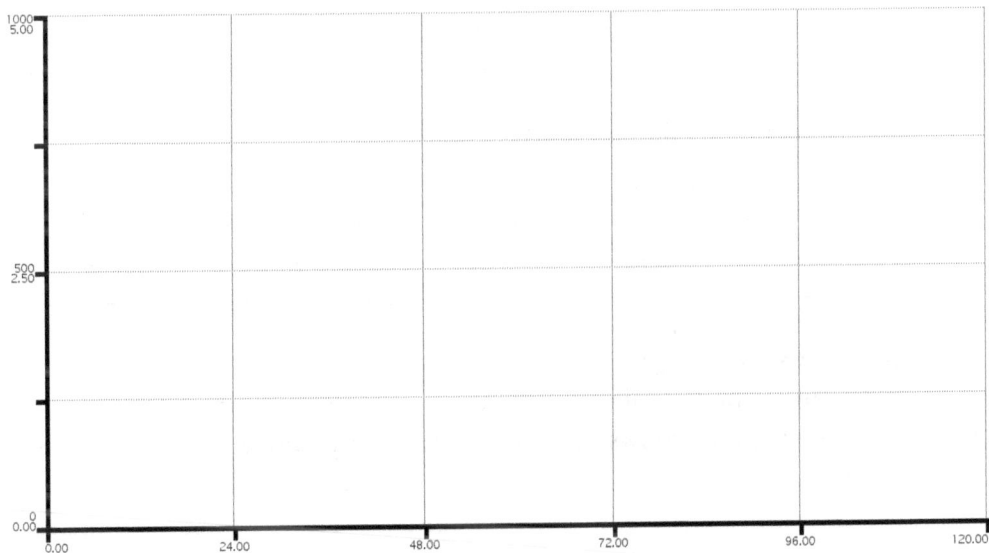

LESSON 7, LEVEL B, HANDOUT 2 – P.6

d. What happened to the availability of pork and retail price over time?
_____
_____
_____
_____

e. Why do you think this occurred? Include specific information about how the farm settings affected the situation.
_____
_____
_____
_____
_____
_____
_____

Click on the bottom-left corner of the graph to see Page two.
f. What happened to the number of piglets, mature hogs, and available pork over time?
_____
_____
_____
_____

g. How do these graphs relate to the retail pork price graph?
_____
_____
_____
_____

Click on the bottom-left corner of the graph to see Page three.
h. Did the farmers make money on the sale of pork over time? Use the graph to explain your response. Notice that the break-even point shows zero profit. Anything above that line is profit. Anything below the line is a loss.
_____
_____
_____
_____
_____
_____
_____

LESSON 7, LEVEL B, HANDOUT 3 – P.1

From Farm to Table – Debrief

Go back to the Menu and **click Debrief**. Explore each of the four sections, answering the questions below.

Click 1. Hog Farm Ups and Downs
Look at each of the comparisons. Make sure to read each of the stories and look at the graphs.

a. Which kind of farm (large or small) was most stable in terms of availability of pork, price, and animals?
_____

Why do you think this is the case? _____
_____
_____

b. Which kind of farm (large or small) was most able to provide food for the most people?
_____

Why do you think this is the case? _____
_____
_____

c. What is your idea for creating a farm that best meets the needs of all?
_____
_____
_____

Click 2. Hog Farm Circles.
a. Read the story of the loop. Why do the loops create ups and downs over time?
_____
_____
_____

b. Draw another loop or loops based on another product.

©2014 Creative Learning Exchange

LESSON 7, LEVEL B, HANDOUT 3 – P.2

Click 3. Hog Farm Map.
Read and follow the directions on this screen.
How did the six parts you changed affect the system over time?

Breeding plan:
_____
_____
_____
_____
_____

Large vs. small farm*:
_____
_____
_____
_____
_____

Pigs that die per 100:
_____
_____
_____
_____
_____

Piglets per litter:
_____
_____
_____
_____
_____

Time to raise:
_____
_____
_____
_____
_____

Additional cost per hog:
_____
_____
_____
_____
_____

* Hint: Large and small farms are not labeled on this map. When you clicked on large or small in the simulation, how did it affect parts that you do see?

Click 4. Connections
a. What are some other connections you can see between product cycles (as you experienced with hog farming) and other systems in the world.

_____
_____
_____
_____
_____
_____
_____

From Farm to Table – Farm Comparison

Category	Large Farms	Small Farms
Number of hogs		
Retail pork price		
Practicality in terms of feeding people		
Impact on the environment		
Living conditions for animals		
Other comparison?		

LESSON 7, LEVEL B, HANDOUT 5

From Farm to Table – Assessment

Describe the story of the loops. Make sure to write about each part and how it affects any other parts.
_____
_____
_____
_____
_____
_____
_____
_____
_____
_____

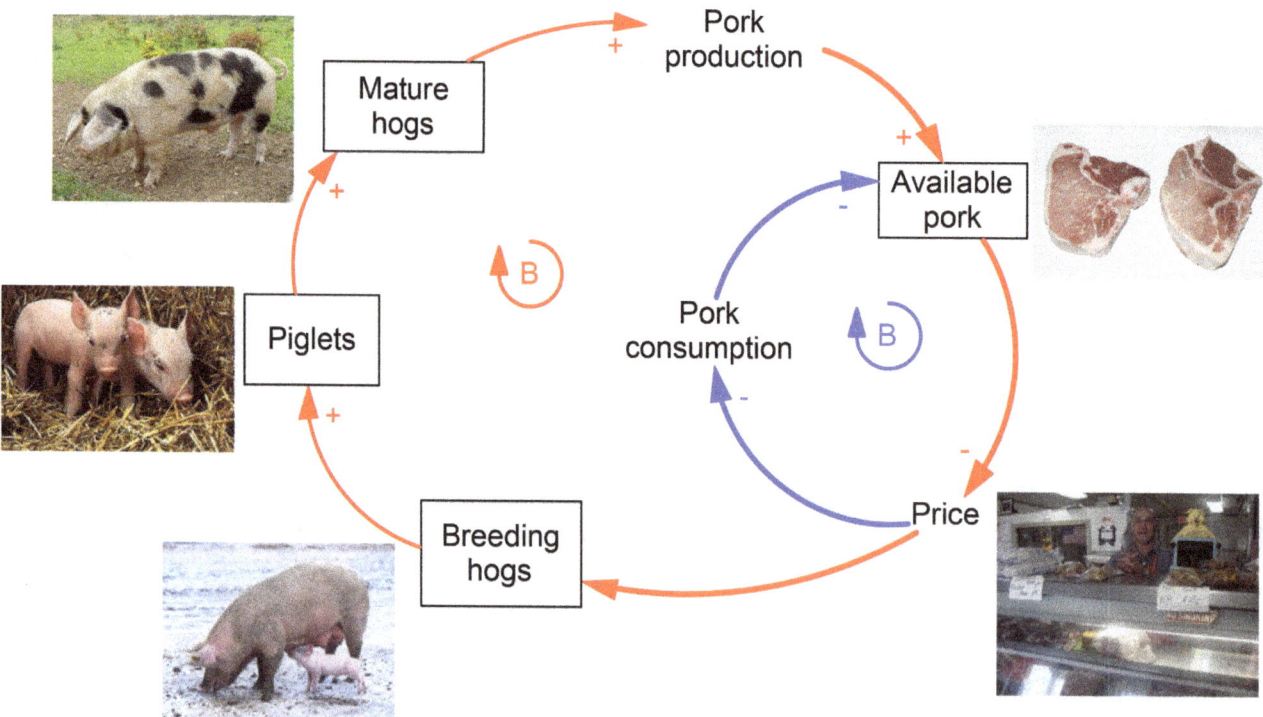

Everything Else

"You can't navigate well in an interconnected, feedback-dominated world unless you take your eyes off short-term events and look for long-term behavior and structure…."

Donella Meadows, *Thinking in Systems*

PHOTO BY ANNE LAVIGNE

Appendix A
Characteristics of Complex Systems

> "The intuitively obvious 'solutions' to social problems are apt to
> fall into one of several traps set by the character of complex systems."
>
> Jay W. Forrester, *World Dynamics*

Complex systems do not always act the way that people intuit. One way to understand the behaviors of these systems is to view them through a lens of common characteristics. Jay Forrester, MIT professor, developed and described these characteristics, given many years of exploring and modeling a variety of complex systems. His statement summarizes the importance of understanding these characteristics when working to address difficult social issues.

What are the characteristics of complex systems? Forrester described seven distinct characteristics (listed here along with additional explanations). The simulations, along with their accompanying materials, most closely demonstrate characteristic #4, although additional characteristics are also strongly embedded in some of the contexts.

Characteristics of Complex Systems

1. Cause and effect are not closely related in time or space.
Complex systems are composed of many interacting feedback loops. They often contain long time delays. What may appear to be an obvious reason for a particular problem is often not the fundamental cause of the problem, but only a symptom.

2. Action is often ineffective due to application of low-leverage policies.
Complex systems contain balancing feedback loops that surround the various goals of the system. Low-leverage policies often seem to be the "obvious" solutions to the problem at hand, but they encounter resistance – the tendency for interventions to be defeated by the response of the system to the intervention. Low-leverage policies are unable to overpower the balancing loops in order to align the competing goals of the system. In this complex system, the symptoms are commonly treated, rather than the problem.

3. High-leverage policies are difficult to apply correctly.
Complex systems contain areas of high leverage – places where a small push in the correct direction is likely to effect the desired change. In many cases, these high-leverage policies are difficult to identify and difficult to apply correctly. The "levers" for such policies may be pushed in the wrong direction, or not pushed at all.

4. The cause of the problem is within the system.
Problems observed in complex systems are almost always internally generated. While it is easier and more comfortable to place blame on others, it is more productive to look within the system itself to understand and change undesirable behavior. This complex system characteristic is often identified by the oscillation of the system.

5. Collapsing goals results in a downward spiral.

Complex systems tend to drift to lower levels of performance over time. This can occur over a long time-frame, making the downward spiral both insidious and hard to combat. This situation occurs when individuals or institutions respond to failing to reach their goals by adjusting them downward in order to relieve the discomfort of failure.

6. Conflicts arise between short-term and long-term goals.

In complex systems, there are tradeoffs between short-term and long-term goals. What is achievable or desirable within a short time-frame can reveal problematic consequences in the fullness of time. Conversely, concentrating on a future payoff almost always involves sacrifice in the present.

7. Burdens are shifted to the intervener.

This characteristic is often closely related to the tradeoff between short-term and long-term goals. Both play out over time, but the presence of an intervener usually means that a form of addiction or dependence is at work. The system's natural ability to fend for itself declines over time as the addiction/dependence becomes stronger.

Appendix B
System Dynamics Visual Tools

Behavior-over-time Graph

The variable being measured is always on the y-axis of the graph. Time is displayed on the x-axis. Depending on the context, the time frame could be short (measured in seconds) or long (measured in years). Most of the models in this series produce a variety of oscillatory behaviors, although other trends are also possible.

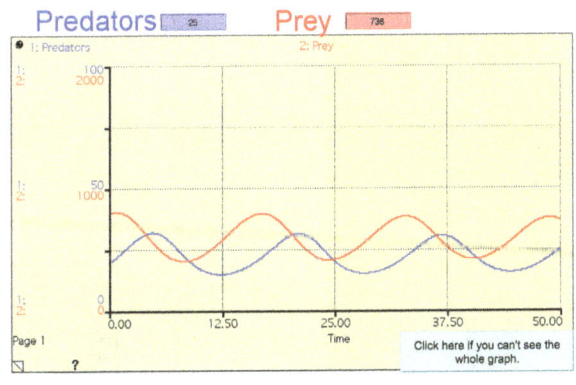

Causal Loop Diagram

A causal (or feedback) loop diagram is another visual tool that shows the structure of a system. A feedback loop tells a story about how a system operates. Any given system may have multiple interconnected loops. Arrows between any two elements indicate a cause-and-effect relationship: If the first element rises, then it causes the second element either to rise or fall. Depending on the relationship, different symbols are used. See the loop below along with the key explaining the different symbols.

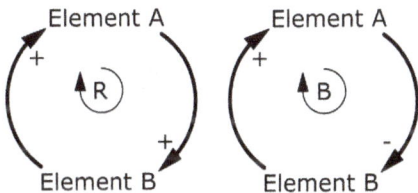

+ indicates a direct or additive relationship between the two elements.
- indicates an indirect or subtractive relationship between the two elements.
R in the middle indicates that the loop reinforces.
B in the middle indicates that the loop balances.

Stock/Flow Map

A stock/flow map represents the structure of the system. The parts of the map along with the underlying mathematical assumptions define the nature of the interdependent relationships among the parts. This structure is based on assumptions about how the system (whether it be a spring or relationships on the playground) really works.

In its simplest form, a stock represents an accumulated amount and the flow (or flows) represent the rate at which the stock goes up or down. Other elements impact one or more flows, either adding to or subtracting from a stock.

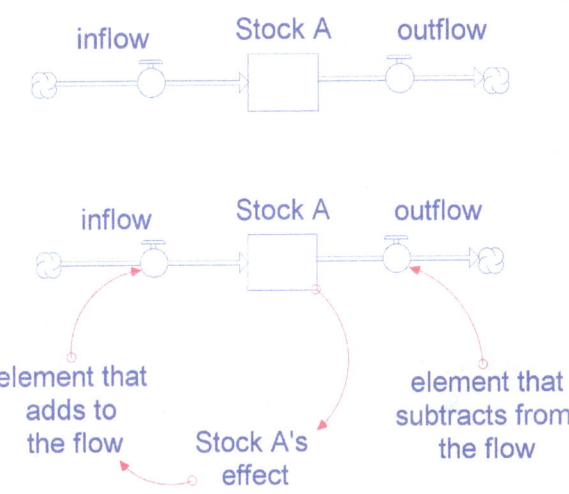

Appendix C
Technical Matters

Setting Up the Simulation

Menu System

Each simulation level has a standardized menu system displayed in a recommended order of use. Handouts guide students through all sections of each level's menu system.

Level A Menu

Level B Menu

| Introduction | Decisions | Simulation Results | Debrief | Next Steps |

Level C Menu Example

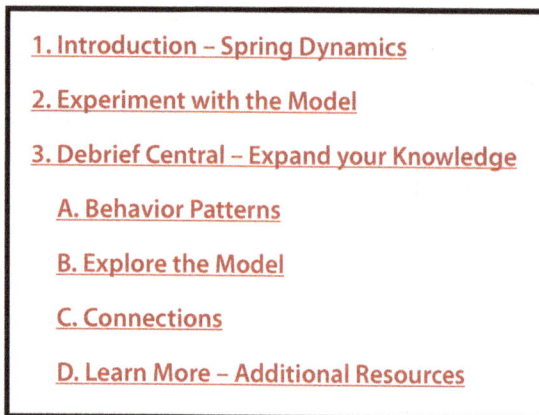

Home

 Every screen has a "Home" button available. This button returns the user to the beginning title screen of the simulation.

Slidebars

Slidebars are one method for manipulating the settings for a simulation. Some of the slidebars have a general range, with no values showing. One example within the Level A – Spring Simulation shows a range of springiness from "easy to pull" to "hard to pull." Other simulations have slidebars that include numerical settings. The lesson handouts might ask the student to set a slidebar to a particular number.

General Range Slidebar   **Specific Numerical Slidebar**

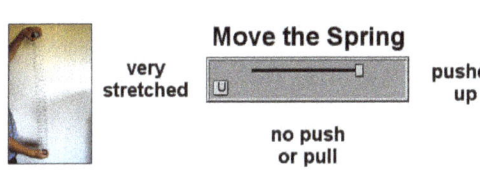   

Initial position

Additional aspects of slidebars include:
- Setting a slidebar is as simple as moving the lever to the right or left to select higher or lower settings.
- Slidebars that have visible numerical values can also be set by clicking on the value in the middle and typing in the desired number.
- Slidebars must be set according the indicated minimum and maximum values. For example, if a range is 0–2000, the user will not be able to type in a value that exceeds 2000.
- Slidebars must be set by certain increments, depending on the variable. For example, if a range is 0–2000, then the increments may go up or down by increments of 100.

Knobs

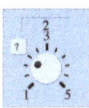 Some of the Level C simulations contain one or more knobs on the control panel screen. These have minimum and maximum values and are set by moving the black dot around to the desired setting.

Buttons

Buttons are used throughout a simulation for different purposes, including navigation among the pages of the simulation, initiating a new simulation run, and resetting the simulation graphs. Depending on the level of the simulation, these buttons may be rectangular images or resemble links on a webpage.

Graphs

Graphs show simulation results as a behavior-over-time graph. The simulation lesson handouts for the B and C levels presume that students know how to create, title, label, and create a key for a line graph.

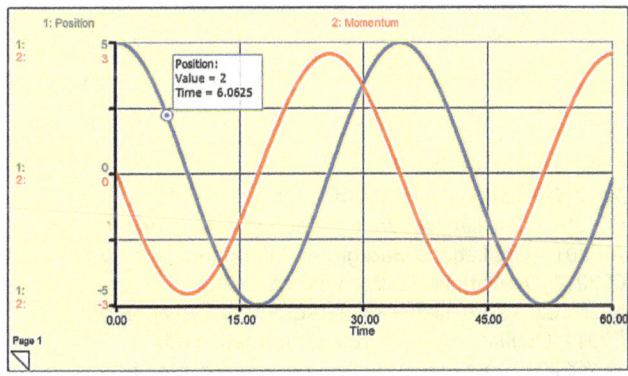

Some graphs may have multiple pages. To see the additional graphs, click on the tab at the bottom, left of the graph pad. Each time you click, the next graph appears. After clicking through all the graphs, the first one will again appear.

To see the actual values at any point on a graph line, click and hold the mouse arrow, right on the line at the point you'd like to check. A box will appear showing the value at a particular point in time.

Troubleshooting

"The simulation gives me a 'time out' message."

When running the simulation online, you may occasionally experience a "time out" message. This can occur for a variety of reasons, but the most common is when nothing on the simulation screen has been clicked for a while. If this happens, simply reload the page and return to the screen you last visited.

"The text and the graphics are all 'mixed up.'"

Occasionally, the development team updates simulations to improve them. If your computer browser has an old version saved in its memory, this can cause the simulation to display erroneous information. To fix this issue, you need to clear the cache from your browser. Browsers (e.g., Internet Explorer, Firefox, Safari) have different procedures for doing this, so see the help documentation for your browser if needed.

"The simulation behavior doesn't make sense."

Each of the simulation models in this series has limitations and is valid only when used within those limitations. If settings that exceed the model parameters are put into the simulation, the user may experience behavior on the graph that doesn't make sense.

For example, the animal population simulation shows the population trends for the animals included on the handouts. If the user tries to input data for an animal that has a very long lifespan and that frequently has many offspring, an exponential growth pattern may be produced. In reality, something else would limit the population growth, but the parameters of the simulation are not able to handle that extreme scenario.

See the accompanying background documents for additional information about the limitations of each model.

"I can't see the entire line on the graph."

In some cases, you may input settings that cause the behavior to go beyond the scale of a particular graph. If this occurs, most of the simulations have a button that allows the user to see the full graph. Note that no scale is set for this special graph, but rather a new scale (on the y-axis) is created with each new run.

"The QR codes are not working."

You can access all the simulations here:
https://exchange.iseesystems.com/profile/25/52

Background documents based on Level C simulations are available here:
Springs- http://static.clexchange.org/ftp/documents/x-curricular/CC2012_Oscillations1BackgroundInformation.pdf
Playground- http://static.clexchange.org/ftp/documents/x-curricular/CC2012_Oscillations2BackgroundInformation.pdf
Population- http://static.clexchange.org/ftp/documents/x-curricular/CC2012_Oscillations3BackgroundInformation.pdf
Pred/prey- http://static.clexchange.org/ftp/documents/x-curricular/CC2012_Oscillations4BackgroundInformation.pdf
Pred/prey/food- http://static.clexchange.org/ftp/documents/x-curricular/CC2012_Oscillations5_BackgroundInformation.pdf
Burnout - http://static.clexchange.org/ftp/documents/x-curricular/CC2012_Oscillations6BackgroundInformation.pdf
Commodities - http://static.clexchange.org/ftp/documents/x-curricular/CC2012_Oscillations7BackgroundInformation.pdf

About Us

About the Authors

Jennifer Andersen is a system dynamics professional who collaborates with the Creative Learning Exchange to create simulations for a wide audience. Since completing her education in simulation modeling fifteen years ago, she has consulted for many projects in the US, Scandinavia, Europe, and South America. She is particularly interested in promoting system dynamics as a tool for understanding complex systems and enhancing formal education in the STEM (Science, Technology, Engineering and Math) disciplines.

Anne LaVigne works with the Creative Learning Exchange and the Waters Foundation. She is a teacher, coach, instructional designer, and most importantly, a learner. For more than twenty years, she has collaborated with educators and students across K-12 settings using systems thinking and system dynamics tools. She strives to develop and share strategies for understanding dynamic, interdependent systems in ways that empower, engage, and motivate.

Lees Stuntz has worked for over twenty years encouraging the use of system dynamics and systems thinking in K-12 education. As Executive Director of the Creative Learning Exchange, she has created and edited multiple pieces of curriculum – available on the Creative Learning Exchange's website (www.clexchange.org), including seven books, as well as numerous curricular units. She collaborates with educators, system dynamicists and citizen advocates toward a collective goal of educating students to be effective systems citizens in our complex world.

The Creative Learning Exchange

The Creative Learning Exchange was founded as a non-profit organization in 1991 to encourage an active, learner-centered process of discovery for 5–19 year-old students that engages in meaningful, real-world problem solving through the mastery of systems thinking and system dynamics modeling. Since its inception, the CLE has worked to encourage teachers and educators to use systems thinking and system dynamics in classrooms and schools throughout the United States, as well as internationally. The CLE has done this through its website that offers free curriculum, its products that include books and games that promote systems thinking, and a biennial conference to help educators and students learn and utilize systems thinking and system dynamics in the classroom and the school organization.

System Dynamics and Jay Forrester

System dynamics is a field of study and a perspective for understanding change. Using computer simulation and other tools, system dynamics looks at how the feedback structure of systems causes the change we observe all around us. System dynamics was developed over fifty years ago by Professor Jay W. Forrester, MIT Professor Emeritus, and is used to address problems in areas ranging from ecology to business management, economics, and psychology. Under Forrester's guidance, system dynamics is helping teachers make K-12 education more learner-centered, engaging, challenging, and relevant to our rapidly changing world.

For more than twenty-five years, Professor Forrester has fostered this work within K-12 education. His direct support allowed the creation of these simulations and accompanying materials, which enables students to explore what are often befuddling characteristics of complex systems.

Led by a partnership between Dr. Forrester and the Creative Learning Exchange, the goal of this ongoing project is to create online curriculum materials for students, aged five and above, to illustrate characteristics of complex systems. In exploring the nature of complex social systems, the materials address questions such as:

- Why do such systems resist policy changes?
- Why are short-term and long-term responses to corrective action often at odds with each other?
- How can leverage points be applied to bring about desirable change in social systems?

The goals of the project are grounded in the belief that an abstract level of understanding of social systems will help prepare future citizens to actively shape their society.

www.ingramcontent.com/pod-product-compliance
Lightning Source LLC
Chambersburg PA
CBHW080444110426
42743CB00016B/3278